Not just what to do, but how to do it!

Action Plan

for Sales

Success

Susan A. Enns

Managing Partner
B2B Sales Connections

ISBN: 978-0-9876928-0-1

DEDICATION

To Dad - You taught me the ever important lesson of persistence.
I have yet to meet anyone who can match your "never give up attitude."
You epitomized the saying "Blessed are those who dream dreams,
and have the guts to make them happen." - Author Unknown

Action Plan For Sales Success

TABLE OF CONTENTS

Chapter 2 - It All Starts Here! Define Your Target Market, Create Your Follow-Up File & Then Prospect! **33**

"Success is simple.
 Do what's right, the right way,
 at the right time." – Arnold Glascow

INTRODUCTION

Congratulations! By purchasing *"Action Plan For Sales Success"* you have taken your next step towards achieving your sales potential! Before we get started, a little about why we are here.

Studies show 25% of sales reps produce 90 to 95% of all sales. Clearly, most sales people are not selling up to their potential, and not making the incomes they could, nor producing the revenues they should.

Why is this case? It's not that the job can't be done because 25 percent are doing it, and doing it well. It's because the other 75 percent either are not in the right sales position or they truly don't know how to sell. If all sales people knew and did what the top 25 percent do, then all sales people would be selling more!

B2B Sales Connections wants to change that. We are an online sales training website with free sales resources, a specialized sales job board and free resume listing services for business to business sales. I guess one could say we specialize in helping b2b sales professionals achieve their sales potential, either by connecting them to the right career choices, or the right skill set. Our website is b2bsalesconnections.com.

My name is Susan A. Enns, and I am Managing Partner of B2B Sales Connections. I have over 22 years of direct sales, management and executive level business to business experience. My accomplishments include being the top sales rep in Canada twice before being promoted to management, managing the top sales branch in the country, and achieving outstanding sales growth in a national channel sales organization. I have written training courses on sales and sales management, created numerous automated sales tools, and my work has been published in several locations numerous times.   I am also currently the President for the Sales Professionals of Ottawa.

The reason for me telling you this is not to toot my own horn. It's just to prove that if I can do it, anyone can! My sales success was not because I am smarter than anyone else. Mind you I have four brothers. If you ever meet them, I will deny I said that.

It was also not because I worked harder than everyone else. True, I did come from a farming family and you do learn a hard work ethic in that environment. The only way you get out of work is if there is an amputation and even then it's only when the bleeding stops. But in reality, most days I had a 5:30 tee off time so my success was not because of super long hours of work.

In reality, my success, like the rest of the sales reps in that top 25% is because I learned how to work smarter, not harder. Someone showed me the right way to do things, and I hope to help you do the same.

"Action Plan For Sales Success" is based on over 50 years of successful B2B sales and sales management expertise. It includes my own personal sales techniques, as well as other successful sales professionals I have been lucky enough to work with over the years.

This is not just a "30,000 foot level" discussion about what to do to sell more. More importantly, this is an action based exercise that will actually show you how! *"Action Plan For Sales Success"* is separated into four sections, each discussing a different stage of the sales process. In each section, we use of specific sales tools and templates. Manual versions of these tools are included here in the appendices located at the end of each section. If you would like to download the automated versions of the tools, you can purchase them in our eStore at www.b2bsalesconnections.com

Together we can all achieve our sales potential! So lets' get started!

Chapter 1 – Why Are You In Sales? Goal Setting & Action Planning

"If you don't know where you are going,
you'll end up someplace else." - Yogi Berra

WHAT IS YOUR GOAL?

A sales representative without a goal is like a ship without a rudder. You will spend a lot of time sailing in circles, but you will never really get closer to where you want to go. A sales rep with a goal but no plan of action on how to achieve it is like a ship's captain without a navigation map. You may be sailing in a straight line, but you may be sailing in completely the wrong direction.

Simply put, when you are in a performance-based career like sales, goal setting is vital to your success. Vital, yes, but without a plan of action on how to achieve your objectives, goal setting is really just an exercise in futility.

So what are your goals? Is it the sales quota that your sales manager assigns to you at the start of the year? Perhaps. True, your minimum acceptable level of sales performance is important, but is it YOUR goal? Is your sales quota important enough for you to hold it dear to your heart and make it the driving force in your life? Probably not.

What you do for a living is a means to an end to achieving what you want in life. In other words, the career that you have chosen is the way in which you earn income to fund the lifestyle that you want to live. That lifestyle is a personal decision, however determining the income required to fund it is your first step in goal setting.

Before going any further, you need to be able to answer the following question: What is the total annual income you wish to earn to fund your desired lifestyle?

The spreadsheet *Personal Goal Definition Worksheet.xls* is an Excel file that will help you answer this question. As you can see, goal setting covers many lifestyle areas and is truly personal in nature. Remember, by signing the form, you are committing to yourself, not anyone else, that you will work towards what you want in life!

B2B SALES CONNECTIONS

Personal Goal Definition Worksheet

Enter information in yellow boxes to define your personal goals.

Step 1 - Personal Commitment	
I am committed to and will work towards achieving my personal goals as listed below.	
Name	Sam Q. Salespro
Date	January 4, 2009 (Today)

Step 2 - Lifestyle & Leisure Time Goals	
Next 12 Months	Spend more time with the family; Golf once per week; Make time for my hobby
Next 2 - 4 Years	Buy a house; Buy a car; Take a winter holiday down south; Season's tickets to local sports team
Long Term	Retire at 55;

Step 3 - Career & Educational Goals	
Next 12 Months	Become B2B Sales Connections Accredited; Make quota; Earn the trip to President's Club
Next 2 - 4 Years	Earn a promotion to sales management; Take audult education course in public speaking
Long Term	Earn a promotion to senior management

Step 4 - Health & Fitness Goals	
Next 12 Months	Work out for 30 minutes per day; Quit smoking
Next 2 - 4 Years	Lose 20 pounds
Long Term	Have an annual checkup; Eat healthy food

Step 5 - Spirtual & Community Involvement Goals	
Next 12 Months	Voluteer at the Hospital; Read 10 minutes a day on Self Improvement
Next 2 - 4 Years	Join a house of worship
Long Term	Earn Coaching Level 1 Certificate

Step 6 - Financial Goals	
Next 12 Months	Get out of credit card debt; Develop a monthly budget
Next 2 - 4 Years	Start an RRSP; Start an TFSA; Invest in the stock market
Long Term	Be mortgage free; Be financially independent

Step 7 - Annual Income Goal		
To fund my desired lifestyle and achieve my goals as outlined above, I must earn an annual income of		$100,000
Signature	Sam Q. Salespro	

WHAT IS YOUR SALES PROCESS?

The next step in goal setting is to convert your total annual income into the daily activities that are required to earn it. The bottom line is that you need to determine what you must do each and every day to ensure that you will reach your desired income at the end of the year.

As your chosen career is sales, the daily activity required to achieve your goal depends on how much you sell, and the process by which you sell it. Different industries use different processes to market their products. Although your sales process may be specific to your industry, every sales process contains three basic steps: prospecting; fact finding; and the presentation of offer stage. Each step leads to the next, where the end result is the sale!

In some transactional sales, the entire sales process may be accomplished in a single call, however many products and services require multiple contacts with the potential customer.

The Prospecting Call

The first step in any sale is the prospecting call. This includes any type of customer contact that attempts to open the sales process. It could include a telemarketing call, a face to face prospecting call, or a follow up call from previous sales contact. It could also include contact as a result of the prospective customer contacting you first, perhaps via your website or the telephone directory. Sometimes, you may even have to do a combination of different kinds of prospecting calls with the same company.

Essentially, any attempt to initiate the sale process is considered a prospecting call. A prospecting call is considered a success if you and your prospective customer agree to proceed to the next step in the sales process.

The Fact Find

The second step in the sales process is the fact find, or information gathering stage. At this stage, you are gathering all the relevant information needed to prepare your offer to the customer. You are identifying the relevant contacts and buying processes within your prospect's organization. You are also determining if sales opportunities actually exist, and if so, what are the time frames of those identified sales opportunities. Again, depending on your industry, a thorough needs analysis may require you to complete more than one fact find appointment at the same company.

Simply put, any sales call that is intended to gather or confirm information about your prospective customer is considered a fact find. A fact find is considered successful if you and your prospect confirm that the sales process should continue to the last step of the sales process.

The Presentation of Offer

The final step in the sales process before completing the sale is the presentation of offer stage. The presentation stage includes any calls that actually present or clarify the offer with the prospect. This could include presenting a written proposal, or an equipment demonstration, or both. It would also include any calls needed to answer any objections your customer may have, or any appointment needed to complete your sales order paperwork.

Any sales call that presents or clarifies what you are selling is considered a presentation. A presentation is successful if you and your prospect agree to proceed to close the sale by the customer ordering your product.

TRACK SALES ACTIVITY TO ENSURE YOUR SUCCESS!

Regardless of your industry or how you market your products, over time you will see that you need to complete a certain number of calls within each step of the sales process to close just one sale.

A sales career is really a profession that lives on the law of averages. Applying these laws with a little basic math, and you can quickly determine what activities you need to commit to each and every day to achieve your own personal goals. However, before we can complete this exercise we must have all the information necessary to make the calculations.

More specifically, in order to calculate the daily activities needed to achieve your goals, you must first know the following information:

- Your total annual income goal
- Your base salary
- Your annual, quarterly or monthly income bonuses, if applicable
- Your average commission rate
- Your average size sale
- The number of presentations it takes you to make a sale
- The number of fact finds it takes you to make a presentation
- The number of prospecting calls it takes you to book a fact find.

Each bit of information is like a piece in a bigger jig saw puzzle, with one piece needing completion before the next piece can be fitted. The end result is the picture of what you need to do to be successful.

You should already know your total annual income goal. You should also already know your base salary. However, you may or may not know the rest of the information required. If you don't know all the information, you either need to find it, estimate it, or create it based on past experience. However you obtain it, the more accurate the information, the better. Remember, you are determining what *you* need to do to make *you* successful. If your information is inaccurate, you are only fooling yourself.

Income Bonuses

Your compensation plan may or may not include some sort of bonus structure. If you do not have any bonuses available to you, you can skip this section. If you do have bonuses available to you, however, you must account for them. In fact, you must account for all sources of income generated from your sales activities. If a source of income is a fixed amount, then you can add it to your base salary figure. An example of this may be a fixed automobile or cellular phone allowance. If the source of income is variable and depends on your sales performance, then it should be accounted for as an available bonus.

If you have been in your position for some time, you should have a good idea as to what bonuses you have earned based on your previous sales performance. A quick look at last December's pay stub or T4 slip should be all that is needed. However, if you are new to sales or your current position, you may need to ask your colleagues or your sales manager what figures you should use. Lastly, you could assume that you will achieve a certain level of bonus attainment, say 75, 100, or 125 percent, and translate that into a bonus income amount.

The bottom line is that all sources of income contribute to the achievement of your income goal, and therefore must be included in your calculations.

Average Commission Rate

Some compensation plans have a fixed commission rate that is paid when a sale is made, while others have a commission rate that is a variable on the product or service sold or the selling price attained. There are many combinations, with as many possibilities as there are B2B sales organizations! The idea here is not to over analyze, but just to find your average commission rate.

Again, if you have been in your position for some time, finding this information should be quite simple. Your average commission rate is simply calculated by dividing the total amount of commission you earned by your total annual sales volume over the same time period. For example, if you earned $50,000 in commissions on a sales volume of $1,000,000, your average commission rate is $50,000/$1,000,000 or 5 per cent. It is not important that some of these commissions were earned at 4 per cent and some at 6 per cent, it is only important that the average was 5 per cent.

You could also ask your colleagues or your sales manager what is the average annual commission rate. If you are new to your position and have not yet had a chance to track your own results to calculate your average commission rate, this may be the only way to estimate the information you need. If you are more experienced, comparing yourself to your peers in this way may be quite eye opening. If your rate is higher than your peers, you are doing something differently that is earning you a higher income. Great job!

Conversely, if your rate is lower, you may want to ask yourself what your colleagues are doing differently than you.

Average Sale Size

Your average sale size is easily calculated by dividing the total sales volume by your total number of sales over the same time frame. For example, if you sold $1,000,000 last year, and you did it by completing 100 sales, your average sale size is $1,000,000/100 or $10,000. Some of these deals may have been very large and some may have been very small. The breakdown of each deal is not important, just the average.

It is also recommended that you talk to your peers and your sales manager. Not only will you see how you compare with others in your company, but you may also gain some valuable insights as to how you can increase you average size sale.

Sales Process Averages

How many presentations does it take to make a sale? How many fact find appointments does it take to make a presentation? How many prospecting calls does it take to book a fact find? These sales process averages are critical when you are calculating the daily activities necessary to achieve your goals, yet very few sales representatives know this information.

If you have not been tracking your sales activity in the past, the best way to estimate these averages is by asking others about theirs. However, individual results can vary greatly by sales representative. For example, many industries like insurance claim they average ten calls to three appointments to one sale. The question that then comes to mind is why isn't every insurance sales representative who makes ten calls making at least one sale?

The answer is because not every sales representative works the same way. Everyone doesn't use the same prospecting approach, and everyone doesn't call on the same prospects. They all don't ask the same questions in their fact finds, nor do they all use the same proposal templates. As such, not every sales representative yields the same averages!

When getting started, you may not have any choice but to depend on the averages of other sales representatives in your company or industry. However, the absolute best way to ensure that you are using accurate information is to track your own sales activities.

How to Track Your Sales Activities

Chances are, as a job requirement, you must submit a weekly sales report to your sales manager. Some sales representatives, normally those who are not at quota, perceive these sales reports as a policing action. "The boss is only checking up on me to ensure that I am doing my prospecting calls". Believe me when I tell you that your sales manager already knows if you are making your calls or not, regardless of whether or not you are submitting a sales report. Your sales results, or lack thereof, are already showing your manager that information.

The most successful sales representatives look at sales reports in a completely different way. They see the reports as tools to monitor if they are on course to reach their goals. These sales representatives know that by tracking their activities, they can ensure that they are completing the necessary daily tasks that will make them successful. They also know that activity tracking can determine areas for improvement so they can be more successful in the future. In other words, the most successful sales representatives, those that make the highest incomes, see sales reports and activity tracking as their GPS navigation system on the road to achieving their income and lifestyle goals.

The spreadsheet *Activity Tracking Worksheet.xls* is an Excel file that tracks your sales activities over a 52 week period. As shown in the example on the next page, as you enter information in the yellow boxes, the spreadsheet will automatically calculate your average commission rate, your average size sale, and your sales process averages.

If you are not familiar with Excel, you can easily track the same information on paper, and then manually calculate the averages. All the forms necessary to do this are included in Appendix A at the end of the training module.

Regardless of your preferred method, in addition to your sales results, it is important to account for your activities at each step of the sales process.

Activity Tracking Worksheet

B B SALES CONNECTIONS

Enter data in yellow boxes each week to calculate your sales process averages.

Your average commission rate	8.00%
Your average sale size	$ 10,000.00
The number of presentations it takes you to make a sale	3.00
The number of fact finds it takes you to make a presentation	2.00
The number of prospecting calls it takes you to book a fact find	15.00

Week Number	Number of Prospecting Calls Completed	Number of Fact Finds Completed	Number of Presentations Completed	Number of Sales Closed	Volume of Sales Closed	Commissions Earned
1	51	3	1	1	$ 12,000.00	$ 1,000.00
2	39	3	2	0	$ -	$ -
3	42	4	2	0	$ -	$ -
4	48	2	1	1	$ 8,000.00	$ 600.00
5						
6						

Over time, based on your own experience, you will see what you need to do at each step of the sales process to close just one sale. Opportunities for improvement in your sales skills will become apparent. You will also see how these averages improve as you hone your selling skills. Lastly, once you have determined your necessary daily activities, tracking them will ensure that you stay on course.

It is importantly to note that these will be your own averages, not just the averages within your company or industry. They reflect the way you sell and the tools that you use. As such, they will be much more accurate than company or industry statistics, and therefore much more helpful in determining what *you* need to do to be successful. More specifically, by tracking your own sales activities, you will have the information necessary to identify what activities *you* need to complete, each and every day, to ensure that *you* achieve your lifestyle and income goals.

WHAT ARE YOUR DAILY ACTIVITIES?

The daily activities required to achieve your lifestyle and income goals are determined by reversing the sales process. In other words, you need to start the process before you close a sale. Therefore, you need to know how many processes you must start so that you close enough sales to reach your income and lifestyle goals.

Reverse The Sales Process

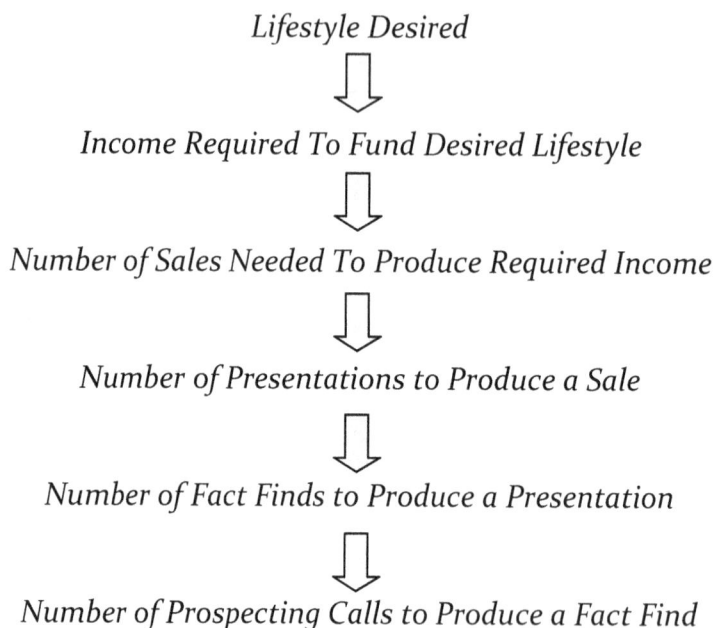

Lifestyle Desired

⇩

Income Required To Fund Desired Lifestyle

⇩

Number of Sales Needed To Produce Required Income

⇩

Number of Presentations to Produce a Sale

⇩

Number of Fact Finds to Produce a Presentation

⇩

Number of Prospecting Calls to Produce a Fact Find

As stated earlier, a sales career is a profession that lives on the law of averages. Now that we have the necessary information, we will use these laws with a little basic math to quickly determine what you need to commit to do each and every day to achieve your own personal goals. How much do you have to sell to reach your goal and earn your desired income? How many proposals do you need to present to sell that amount? How many fact find appointments does this require? How many prospecting calls does this equate to?

The spreadsheet *Goal Setting & Action Planning Worksheet.xls* is an Excel file that will calculate this automatically for you. Enter the data in the yellow boxes and the end result will be what you need to do each day to achieve your goals. This is shown in the example on the following page.

Goal Setting & Action Planning Worksheet

B B SALES CONNECTIONS

Enter data in yellow boxes to calculate the daily activities required to achieve your goals.	
What is the total annual income you wish to earn to fund your lifestyle?	$ 100,000.00
What is your base salary?	$ 50,000.00
What is your average monthly bonus earned?	$ 500.00
What is your average commission rate?	8%
What is your average size sale?	$ 10,000.00
How many presentations does it take you to make a sale?	3.0
How many fact finds does it take you to make a presentation?	2.0
How many prospecting calls does it take you to book a fact find?	15.0
Total Annual Sales Volume Required for Goal Attainment	$ 550,000.00
Total Monthly Sales Volume Required for Goal Attainment	$ 45,833.33
Number of Sales Required Per Month	5
Number of Sales Required Per Week	1.25
Number of Presentations Required Per Month	15
Number of Presentations Required Per Week	3.75
Number of Fact Finds Required Per Month	30
Number of Fact Finds Required Per Week	7.50
Number of Prospecting Calls Required Per Month	450
Number of Prospecting Calls Required Per Week	113
Number of Prospecting Calls Required Per Day	23

If you are not familiar with Excel, you can determine your required daily activities by just filling in the form contained in Appendix A.

Achieving the larger goal of your desired income is made much easier when you know what you need to do each and every day. In other words, completing a daily activity is much easier than achieving an annual target. By breaking out a larger task into the daily activities need to achieve it, you greatly increase your chances of getting to where you want to go!

If you were the sales representative in the example above, it is very important to note that, based on your sales skills and activity history, you must complete 23 prospecting calls a day to achieve your goals. Your success is really nothing more complicated than that. Once you know what must be done each day, it then just becomes a matter of doing it!

WHAT IS YOUR SALES FUNNEL?

Normally, sales people do not wait until they close one sale before starting another. In fact, they will have many potential sales on the go, all at different stages of the sales process. Some opportunities are still in the prospecting stage waiting to begin the sales process. Others have had completed fact finds, but have yet to receive the offer presentation. While still others have received the offer presentation and all that is left to complete the sale is the paperwork.

A graphic representation of this is commonly referred to as the Sales Funnel. Your potential sales opportunities are poured into the top of the funnel, and as each one follows your sales process, the funnel narrows, until finally you sales pour out of the bottom.

The B2B Sales Funnel

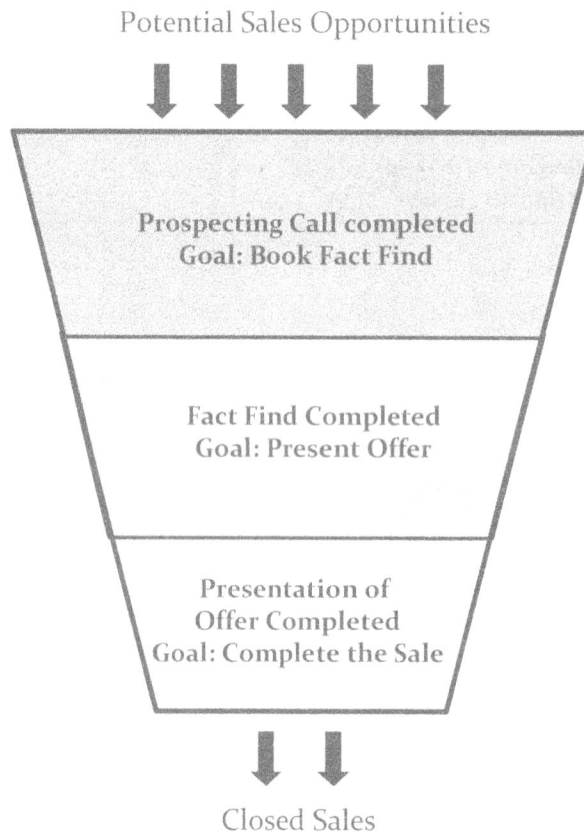

Potential Sales Opportunities

**Prospecting Call completed
Goal: Book Fact Find**

Fact Find Completed
Goal: Present Offer

Presentation of
Offer Completed
Goal: Complete the Sale

Closed Sales

Ensuring that you always have a sufficient number of potential sales entering and exiting your sales funnel is commonly referred to as Sales Funnel or Pipeline Management. By using your sales process averages calculated earlier, you can determine the total number and dollar value of sales that you need at each level of the sales funnel to achieve your goals.

For example, if you were the sales rep who completed the *Activity Tracking Worksheet.xls* shown earlier, you would have determined that you need three presentations to make a sale, two fact finds to make a presentation, and fifteen prospecting calls to make a fact find. Entering this information into your *Goal Setting & Action Planning Worksheet.xls*, you would have determined that you need to sell a monthly volume of $45,833 to achieve your overall income goals.

It is important to note that these sales process ratios hold true for the number of sales required and the dollar value of sales required. Therefore, in order to reach your monthly sales objective, with a presentation to sales ratio of three to one, you need to have $137,499 ($45,833 x 3) in the "Presentation Completed" level of your sales funnel.

By tracking your sales opportunities at each step of the sales process, you can see if you have a healthy sales funnel. In other words, you will see if you have enough in your pipeline at each step of the sales process to ensure you reach your goals.

The spreadsheet *Sales Funnel Management Worksheet.xls* is an Excel workbook that will track this information for you automatically. First, enter all your prospects in the yellow boxes on the worksheet "Sales Funnel Prospects". There are only three options that can be entered for the sales process step completed: Fact Find, Presentation and Sales completed. If you click in a box in this column, a drop down menu will appear so that you can just select one of the three choices.

B SALES CONNECTIONS	Sales Funnel Prospects	
Enter data in yellow boxes each week to calculate your sales process averages. At the end of each month, delete all completed sales.		
Company	Last Step of the Sales Process Completed?	Value of Potential Sale
ABC Company	Fact Find	$ 24,942.00
Profit Inc.	Presentation	$ 5,235.00
Super Sales Rep Corp.	Sale Completed	$ 7,565.00

As you enter your prospects, the spreadsheet will calculate the dollar value of all the prospects in each step of the sales process. The results will appear in the worksheet "Funnel Management Worksheet". This worksheet also creates your target sales funnel based on your sales process averages.

B2B SALES CONNECTIONS

Sales Funnel Management Worksheet

Enter data in yellow boxes each week to calculate your sales process averages.

Your Monthly Sales Objective	$ 45,833.00
The number of presentations it takes you to make a sale	3.00
The number of fact finds it takes you to make a presentation	2.00

Sales Funnel Targets	Sales Process Step	Sales Funnel Actuals
$ 274,998.00	Fact Finds Completed	$ 302,945.00
$ 137,499.00	Presentations Completed	$ 153,940.00
$ 45,833.00	Sales Completed	$ 52,000.00

If you are not familiar with Excel, you can also determine your sales funnel by just filling in the forms contained in Appendix A.

By comparing your target sales funnel to you actual sales funnel, you can see if you are on target to reach your goals. Using your averages, you can actually forecast your future sales over a given time frame. The example above shows a healthy sales funnel. There are sufficient prospects at each level of the sales process to support the next stage, and the end result should be the attainment of your monthly sales objective.

However, perhaps the worksheet shows that you do not have enough prospects at the presentation stage to achieve your monthly sales target. You would therefore need to move more of your potential sales from the fact find stage to the presentation stage as soon as possible. Or perhaps the worksheet shows that you do not have enough customers at the fact find stage. You would therefore need to add more prospects into the top of your sales funnel immediately to ensure that you stay on track.

Knowledge is power. Knowing exactly where you stand, and more importantly if you need to make changes to get back on course, is more than half the battle in getting to where you want to go.

CONCLUSION

The reason many of you chose to pursue sales as your career is that performance based employment gives you the control to earn whatever income is required to live your desired lifestyle. Simply stated, this training module has dealt with what you must do in B2B sales to be successful on your own terms. It has also given you the tools to do it.

Essentially, you are a house builder who has just been given a new tool that will make you much more successful than you have been in the past. Now go swing the hammer! Remember, the only difference between a good idea and a great idea is implementation!

Now that you know what to do, the next step is to learn how to do it, and learn how to do it better.

APPENDIX – MANUAL CALCULATION FORMS

For those of you who are not familiar with Excel spreadsheets, all the calculations discussed in this training module can also be done manually. Simply print the forms on the following pages and follow the instructions.

Excel is a very common business software program. It is highly recommended that you take the time to learn the basics. Not only will you find that it can make your life much easier, you will find it to be a very profitable business tool as well.

Personal Goal Definition
Worksheet

Step 1 - Personal Commitment	
I am committed to and will work towards achieving my personal goals as listed below.	
Name	
Date	

Step 2 - Lifestyle & Leisure Time Goals	
Next 12 Months	
Next 2 - 4 Years	
Long Term	

Step 3 - Career & Educational Goals	
Next 12 Months	
Next 2 - 4 Years	
Long Term	

Step 4 - Health & Fitness Goals	
Next 12 Months	
Next 2 - 4 Years	
Long Term	

Step 5 - Spirtual & Community Involvement Goals	
Next 12 Months	
Next 2 - 4 Years	
Long Term	

Step 6 - Financial Goals	
Next 12 Months	
Next 2 - 4 Years	
Long Term	

Step 7 - Annual Income Goal	
To fund my desired lifestyle and achieve my goals as outlined above, I must earn an annual income of	
Signature	

Activity Tracking Worksheet

Your average commission rate (Total Commissions Earned / Total Volume of Sales Closed)

Your average size sale (Total Volume of Sales Closed / Total Number of Sales Closed)

The number of presentations it takes you to make a sale (Total Number of Presentations / Total number of Sales Closed)

The number of fact finds it takes you to make a presentation (Total Number of Fact Finds / Total Number of Presentations)

The number of prospecting calls it takes you to book a fact find (Total Number of Prospecting Calls / Total number of Fact Finds)

Week Number	Number of Prospecting Calls Completed	Number of Fact Finds Completed	Number of Presentations Completed	Number of Sales Closed	Volume of Sales Closed	Commissions Earned
1						
2						
3						
4						
5						
6						
7						
8						
9						
10						
11						
12						
13						
14						
15						
16						
17						
18						
19						
20						
21						
22						
23						
24						
25						
26						
27						
28						
29						
30						
31						
32						
33						
34						
35						
36						
37						
38						
39						
40						
41						
42						
43						
44						
45						
46						
47						
48						
49						
50						
51						
52						
Totals						

Goal Setting & Action Planning Worksheet

1. What is the total annual income you wish to earn to fund your lifestyle?
2. What is your base salary?
3. What is your average monthly bonus earned?
4. Amount of commission income required to reach annual income goal. (#1-(#2 + #3))
5. What is your average commission rate?
6. Total annual sales volume required. ((#4 / #5) x 100)
7. Monthly sales volume required. (#6 / 12)
8. What is you average size of sale?
9. Total number of sales required per month. (#7 / #8)
10. Total number of sales required per week. (#9 / 4)
11. How many presentations does it take you to make a sale?
12. Number of presentations required per month. (#9 x #11)
13. Number of presentations required per week. (#12 / 4)
14. How many fact finds does it take you to make a presentation?
15. Number of fact finds required per month. (#13 x #14)
16. Number of fact finds required per week. (#15 / 4)
17. How many prospecting calls does it take you to book a fact find?
18. Number of prospecting calls required per month. (#15 x #17)
19. Number of prospecting calls required per week. (#18 / 4)
20. Number of prospecting calls required per day. (#19 / 5)

Sales Funnel
Prospects

Company	Last Step of the Sales Process Completed?	Value of Potential Sale

Sales Funnel Management Worksheet

Your Monthly Sales Objective

The number of presentations it takes you to make a sale

The number of fact finds it takes you to make a presentation

Sales Funnel Targets	Sales Process Step	Sales Funnel Actuals
$ - (Your Monthly Value for Presentations Below X The Number of Fact Finds to Make a Presentation)	Fact Finds Completed	$ - (The Total of Fact Finds Completed from Sales Funnel Prospects Form)
$ - (Your Monthly Sales Objective X The Number of Presentations to Make a Sale)	Presentations Completed	$ - (The Total of Presentations Completed from Sales Funnel Prospects Form)
$ - (Your Monthy Sales Objective)	Sales Completed	$ - (The Total of Sales Completed from Sales Funnel Prospects Form)

Chapter 2 - It All Starts Here!
Define Your Target Market,
Create Your Follow-Up File & Then Prospect!

"Success is simple. Do what's right, the right way,
at the right time." - Arnold Glascow

WHAT IS YOUR TARGET MARKET?

In B2B sales, your target market is simply defined as where you are most likely to find prospects to buy your product or service. In other words, where should you target your prospecting efforts, so that you will most likely find organizations that may buy your particular product, so that you have the greatest chance of making a sale today?

It is dangerous to believe that any company can and will buy from you. You could work very hard at trying, but in the end you will just be wasting time and effort. For example, it is unlikely that you will sell restaurant equipment to a retail clothing store. You could make many prospecting calls trying, but in the end you would just be spinning your wheels. Therefore, you need a more specific definition of your target market so that you can focus your efforts where you are most likely to be successful.

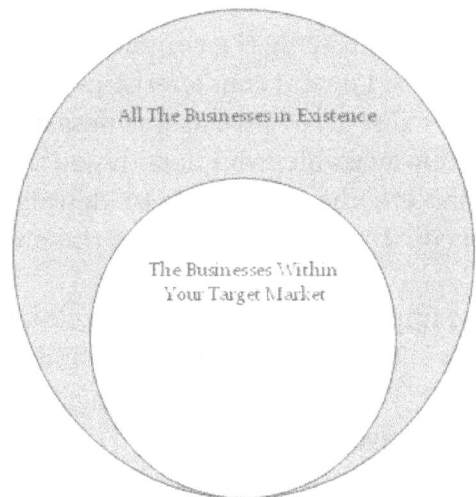

All The Businesses in Existence

The Businesses Within
Your Target Market

Who Are Your Customers?

In order for you to find what types of organizations may buy from you in the future, you need to know what types of organizations have bought from you in the past. When you know this information, you have begun the process to define where you should focus your prospecting efforts.

Every customer that has ever bought your product or service has something in common. Obviously the use of your product itself is a common characteristic, but there are always some other underlying commonalities that result in the use of your product in the first place. They key to specifying your target market is to identify these commonalities so you can find other companies that share them. These are the companies where you want to focus your prospecting and marketing activities as it is with these companies that you will have the greatest chance to make a sale.

If you have been in your position for some time, you may have a good idea as to what are some of the characteristics that your customers all have in common. However, if you are new to sales or your current position, you may need to ask your colleagues or your sales manager. Having said that, opinions, either that of your colleagues or your own, are only estimates. The best method to determine the commonalities that define your target market is to actually analyze past sales.

Unlike when you analyzed your daily activities in Section 1, when analyzing past sales, the bigger the sample size, the better. If you can obtain data for all the sales representatives in your office, or even better, all the sales representatives in your company, this will provide you with very valuable information. Perhaps other representatives are having success in markets that you did not even know existed. You could also speak to your company's marketing department. They may already be tracking this information to use for advertising purposes.

When identifying the commonalities that define your target market, it is best to start with the most general characteristics firsts. These characteristics are most often identified from external sources such as business directories or phone books. The information needed is readily available from outside sources, often at little or no cost to you.   Once this is complete, the next step is to identify common characteristics about your customers that are specific to your company and the products that you sell.

The important commonalities to identify when defining your target market include:
- The types of business or industries in which your customers operate
- The size of your customers based on the number of employees and/or their annual revenue
- The product or product category that the customer purchased from you.
- How much or how often your customers use your product or service.
- Competitive suppliers that your customers used prior to purchasing your product.
- Other products that your customers use that are related to your products
- Any other commonality amongst your customers that you can define.

The spreadsheet *Target Market Definition Worksheet.xls* is an Excel workbook that will help you to determine your target market. The first spreadsheet in the workbook, "Characteristics Worksheet", is a spreadsheet used to create a list of possible choices for each of the different commonalities mentioned above. In other words, it will help you to create a list to which you will compare your current customers, therefore determining their commonalities and your target market definition.

B²B SALES CONNECTIONS

Target Market Characteristic Worksheet

Enter data in yellow boxes to create your Target Market Characteristic Definitions

Number	Type of Business Listing	Number of Employees Listing	Annual Revenue Listing	Product Category Purchased Listing	Product Usage Listing	Previous Supplier Listing	Related Product Listing	Other Commonality Listing #1	Other Commonality Listing #2
1	11 - Agriculture, Forestry, Fishing, and Hunting	Unknown	Unknown	Widget 1	Low Volume	Non User	None		
2	21 - Mining	1 – 4	Less than $500,000	Widget 2	Medium Volume	Unknown Supplier	Gadget 1		
3	22 - Utilities	5 – 9	$500,000 to $1 Million	Widget 3	High Volume	Competitor 1	Gadget 2		
4	23-Construction	10 – 19	$1 Million to $2.5 Million	Widget 4		Competitor 2	Gadget 3		
5	31 to 33 - Manufacturing	20 – 49	$2.5 Million to $5.0 Million	Widget 5		Competitor 3	Gadget 4		
6	42 - Wholesale Trade	50 – 99	$5.0 Million to $10.0 Million			Competitor 4			
7	44 to 45 - Retail Trade	100 – 249	$10 Million - $20 Million			Competitor 5			
8	48 to 49 - Transportation and Warehousing	250 – 499	$20 Million to $50 Million						
9	51 - Information	500 – 999	$50 Million to						
10	52 - Finance and Insurance	1,000 – 4,999	$100 Million to $500 Million						
11	53 - Real Estate and Rental and Leasing	5000 – 9,999	$500 Million to $1 Billion						
12	54 - Professional, Scientific and Technical Services	Over 10,000	Over $1 Billion						
13	55 - Management of Companies and Enterprises								
14	56 - Administrative and Support and Waste Management and Remediation Services								
15	61 - Educational Services								
16	62 - Health Care and Social Assistance								
17	71 - Arts, Entertainment and Recreation								
18	72 - Accommodation and Food Services								
19	81 - Other Services (except Public Administration)								
20	92 - Public Administration								

For those of you not familiar with Excel, you can also do this by filling in the form contained in Appendix A.

When you combine the external information with internal information that is specific to your own customers, you will have a very clear picture as to who has purchased from you in the past, so that you can find similar companies to buy from you in the future.

Type of Business

Identifying the industries in which your customers operate is the first step in defining your target market. But in order to do this for each of your customers, you first must identify a list of all the possible industries to choose from. The most common list available is the telephone directory titles in your local phone book. These can be very specific and the information is free.

Another way to create a list of all the possible industries in which your customers may operate is through the use of Standard Industrial Classification (SIC) codes. This is a system developed by the United States government to categorize all businesses by their primary business activity by assigning each organization a four-digit code. For example, SIC 5511 is the category for all *Motor Vehicle Dealers (New and Used)*.

However times have changed since the system of SIC codes was established in the 1930s. Therefore, it is being phased out by North American Industry Classification (NAICS) system. Released in 1997, NAICS codes are now six digits, and include Canadian and Mexican businesses as well those in the United States. More importantly, they reflect the new and emerging industries, services, and advanced technologies of today's businesses.

A listing of the major business groups within the NAICS and SIC codes are found in the table on the next page. Every type of business that exists, and therefore every one of your customers, could be classified into one of these industry categories. More specific listings of industries found within each major grouping of the NAICS and SIC codes are readily available on the internet. Two excellent websites for further details are:

- http://www.census.gov/epcd/www/naicstab.htm
- http://www.naics.com/search.htm

NAICS Codes		SIC Codes	
Codes	Industry Title	Codes	Industry Title
11	Agriculture, Forestry, Fishing, and Hunting	01-09	Agriculture, Forestry, and Fisheries
21	Mining	10-14	Mineral Industries
22	Utilities	15-17	Construction Industries
23	Construction	20-39	Manufacturing
31-33	Manufacturing	40-49	Transportation, Communications, and Utilities
42	Wholesale Trade	50-51	Wholesale Trade
44-45	Retail Trade	52-59	Retail Trade
48-49	Transportation and Warehousing	60-67	Finance, Insurance, and Real Estate
51	Information	70-89	Service Industries
52	Finance and Insurance	91-99	Public Administration
53	Real Estate and Rental and Leasing		
54	Professional, Scientific and Technical Services		
55	Management of Companies and Enterprises		
56	Administrative and Support and Waste Management and Remediation Services		
61	Educational Services		
62	Health Care and Social Assistance		
71	Arts, Entertainment and Recreation		
72	Accommodation and Food Services		
81	Other Services (except Public Administration)		
92	Public Administration		

Depending on your product or service, you may need a more specific list than these major categories to define your target market. For example, the product you sell may be a type of store fixture for retail stores. Using the NAICS system, all retail stores are classified under the major business group *Retail Trade,* codes 44 to 45. However, there are many different types of retail stores, only a few of which would use your type of store fixture. Therefore, you would want a more detailed type of business listing so that you can better define your target market. In this case, you would use all six digits of the NAICS code to specifically define the types of retail stores in which your customers operate; codes 448110 *Men's Clothing Stores* and 448120 *Women's Clothing Stores*, for example.

Regardless of the list for the types of businesses that you use, it should be relevant to your industry and your product. It should be big enough to show all of the potential industries in which your customers operate, yet not too big to include industries where you will never make a sale. It is recommended that your list be limited to a maximum of fifty types of businesses. Most importantly, the list must be exhaustive. In other words, each of your current and potential customers must be able to be classified by their type of business using the categories contained in your list.

Size of Business

Once you have defined the list of the types of industries that your customers operate in, the next step is to define the list of the sizes of your customers based on the number of employees and/or their annual revenue. Business directories often include this information on the companies they have listed. Another source of this information would be mailing list brokers.

Different sizes of organizations within the same industry have different needs, and as such will affect the way you define your target market. A law firm with one lawyer would have different photocopier needs than a larger firm of 50 lawyers just because of the different number of employees within the office. Also, because of the different level of revenues generated, each law firm would have very different needs for accounting software. Therefore these two law firms would probably be considered two different target markets.

Again, when creating your list(s) to classify your customers by the size of their business, it is important that the list is relevant to your industry, and that every customer must be able to be classified within it. Examples of exhaustive lists for the size of businesses are outlined on the next page.

Unlike the other target market characteristics, where the information is readily available, sometimes information on the size of business is more difficult to determine, or is too expensive to obtain. For example, you can easily determine the type of business for your customer by simply looking them up in the telephone book to see the yellow page category heading. However to determine the annual revenue of that same customer may require paying a business directory or mailing list broker for that information. If the size of business cannot be estimated, then it is best to add to your list a choice like *Unknown*. Knowing this information will give you a better picture of your target market, however sometimes it is just not possible.

Size of Business	
Number of Employees	Annual Revenue
Unknown	Unknown
1 – 4	Less than $500,000
5 – 9	$500,000 to $1 Million
10 – 19	$1 Million to $2.5 Million
20 – 49	$2.5 Million to $5.0 Million
50 – 99	$5.0 Million to $10.0 Million
100 – 249	$10 Million - $20 Million
250 – 499	$20 Million to $50 Million
500 – 999	$50 Million to $100 Million
1,000 – 4,999	$100 Million to $500 Million
5000 – 9,999	$500 Million to $1 Billion
Over 10,000	Over $1 Billion

Product Categories

The next step in defining your target market is to create a list of all the products that you sell. One of the easiest ways to create this list is to simply use the product category headers from your price book. If the product categories are too broad and general, you can define your list in more detail as needed. A good example of this is the office equipment industry. A general product category of *Photocopiers* may be too broad, and perhaps should be broken down into *Photocopiers – Black & White* and *Photocopiers – Colour*.

Like all the other lists created to classify your customers so far, this list must be exhaustive. It must include every product that your customers could possibly buy, but not be too large so that the list becomes unmanageable. A maximum of fifty products or product categories is recommended.

Product Usage

How much or how often a customer uses your product is very important when defining your target market. For example, if you sell faxes, it would be important to know how many faxes your customer sends. Or if you sell pension plans, it would be important to know how many plan members or employees would be covered. Of if you sold water coolers to offices, it would be important to know how many bottles of water that an office consumes in a given time frame.

Defining a list for product usage is very industry specific and depends heavily on the actual products that you sell. It could be very simple, with a broad definition of usage such as low, medium and high. Or it could more specific such as a range of specified volumes per month, such as less than 10, 11 to 19, and more than 20. Regardless of your choices, the list must be exhaustive. Every volume that your customer could use must be able to be categorized by the choices on your list.

Previous Supplier

A list of the competitive suppliers that your customers used prior to purchasing your product is very important when defining your target market. You may find that you win more deals against a certain supplier more often than another. Or you may find that your customers did not have a previous supplier in the first place. Either way, it is important to know this when you begin to look for new customers that share commonalities with your current customers.

Who are your competitors? A simple way to determine this is to look your own company up in the yellow pages. The other companies listed under the same heading are generally your competitors. You could also ask your peers or your sales manager for this information, as they generally have a good idea as to whom you will compete against.

Like all others, this list must be exhaustive, and include every possibility of your customers' previous suppliers. As such, you list should always include two choices. The first is Non User as you may be the first supplier the customer has ever used. The second is Unknown Supplier, as you may know that the customer did have a previous supplier, but the information as to who that supplier was is not available.

Related Products

Sometimes your customers use products or services that are related to the products that you sell. Identifying these types of commonalities is extremely useful when defining your target market. For example, if your product is a software add-on that can only be used with another certain software program, then you would want to track the use of that program. Or, if you are selling group benefit plans, it would be important to know that all of your pension plan customers also had group health and dental plans prior to purchasing the pension plan. Or, if you sell office equipment, it is helpful to know that all of your copier customers also had laser printers and fax machines.

Creating a list of related products is very industry specific. In fact, your list may not be exhaustive when you first create it. Now that you are looking for them, you may discover new related products as you go, and then you can add them to your list later. Depending on your industry, related products may not even exist in the first place. However, if one or more related products can be defined, they can be extremely powerful in defining your target market.

Other Commonalities

Lastly, other commonalities or common characteristics could exist between your customers that are so industry specific that they are beyond the scope of this training course. It is recommended that you ask other sales representatives or your sales manager to see if there are some other commonalities that you should be tracking. If this is the case with your customers, define those commonalities as we have with the other categories above. The more common characteristics you can find among your current customers, the better the definition of your target market. The better the definition of your target market, the more likely the possibility of finding potential customers that exist within it.

Compare Your Customers To Your Commonalities

The last step in defining your target market is to compare your customers to the common characteristics lists that you have developed. In other words, the lists that you have created are how to categorize each of your customers. Now you must actually compare each customer to these lists. By doing so, you will be creating your actual target market definition.

Again, the spreadsheet *Target Market Definition Worksheet.xls* is the Excel workbook that you have been using to help you to determine your target market. The first spreadsheet in the workbook, "Characteristics Worksheet", is where the lists of possible choices for each of the different commonalities were entered. By doing so, this started the comparison process in the second spreadsheet, "Definition Worksheet".

Here is where you enter in your past customer sales and their dollar volume. You also complete the information on each characteristic for each customer. In each characteristic column, drop down arrows will appear when you select the cell. These drop downs include the characteristic lists that you created earlier and you simply click on your selection to enter the information. This way, in order to categorize each of your customers, you must use the lists you have developed.

You can enter in two thousand customers into the spreadsheet to help create your target market definition. The more customers you enter in the better, as this will give you the most accurate picture of where you have sold to in the past, so that you can do so again in the future.

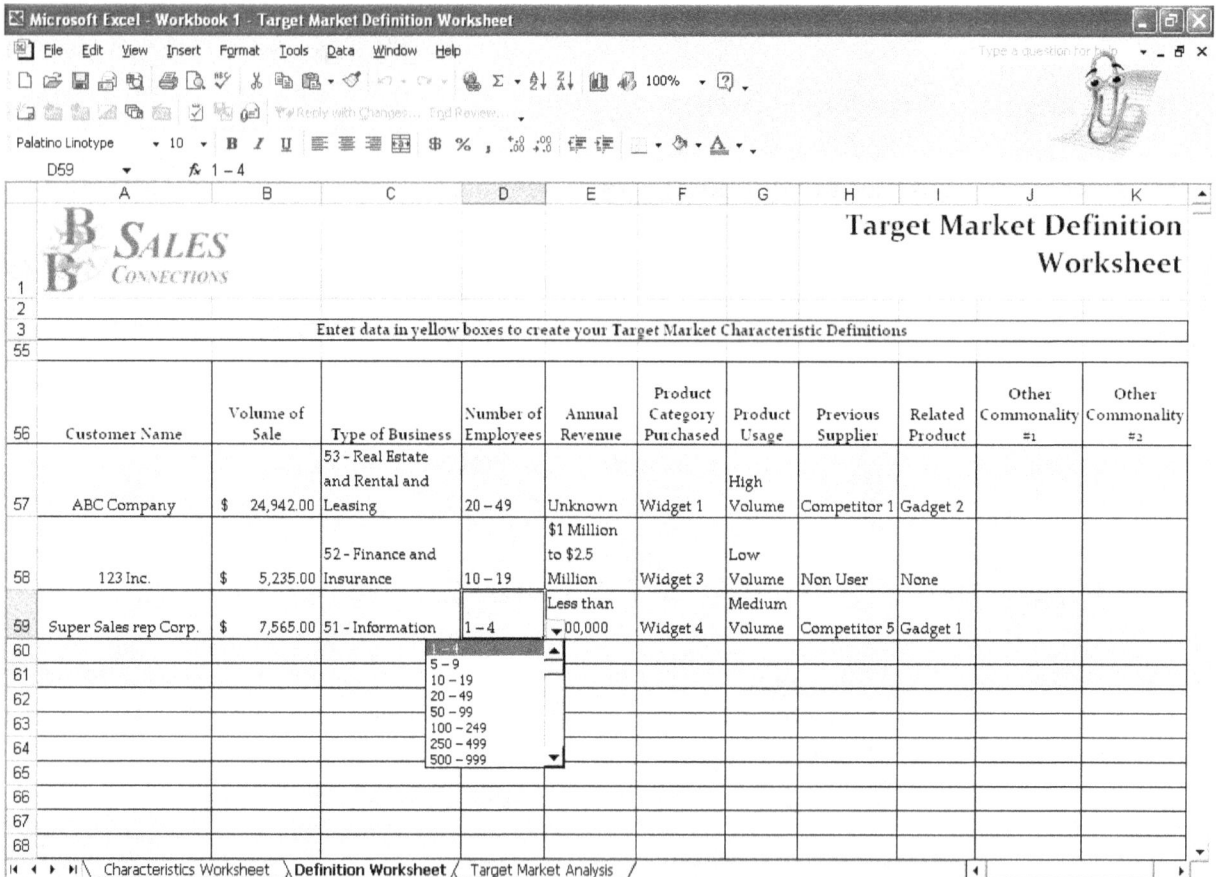

For those of you not familiar with excel, you can do the same analysis manually using the forms found in Appendix A.

As you enter in each past customer sale, the spreadsheet is totaling up the data, and the results are being tallied automatically on the spreadsheet, "Target Market Analysis". For each characteristic, the spreadsheet calculates the number of customers and the total dollar value of sales that match the criteria. Also, the percentage of the total is automatically calculated. To view other characteristics, simply click on the drop down arrow in the yellow box labeled "Class of Characteristic" and select the characteristic you want to view.

Microsoft Excel - Workbook 1 - Target Market Definition Worksheet

File Edit View Insert Format Tools Data Window Help

B4 ='Characteristics Worksheet'!B6

Target Market Definition Analysis

Class of Characteristic	Characteristic	Customer Count	Sales Volume	Customer Count Percentage	Sales Volume Percentage
(All) (Top 10...) (Custom...) Annual Revenue Number of Employees Other Commonality #1 Other Commonality #2 Previous Supplier Product Category Purchased Product Usage Related Product Type of Business	11 - Agriculture, Forestry, Fishing, and Hunting	0	$ -		
	21 - Mining	0	$ -		
	22 - Utilities	2	$ 32,507.00	20%	29%
	23 - Construction	0	$ -		
	31 to 33 - Manufacturing	0	$ -		
	42 - Wholesale Trade	0	$ -		
	44 to 45 - Retail Trade	0	$ -		
	48 to 49 - Transportation and Warehousing	0	$ -		
	51 - Information	1	$ 5,678.00	10%	5%
	52 - Finance and Insurance	6	$ 39,043.00	60%	35%
	53 - Real Estate and Rental and Leasing	1	$ 34,509.00	10%	31%
	54 - Professional, Scientific and Technical Services	0	$ -		
	55 - Management of Companies and Enterprises	0	$ -		
	56 - Administrative and Support and Waste Management and Remediation Services	0	$ -		
	61 - Educational Services	0	$ -		
	62 - Health Care and Social Assistance	0	$ -		

Characteristics Worksheet / Definition Worksheet \ **Target Market Analysis** /

Ready

start   Section 2 - It All Start...   Section 2 - It Starts H...   Microsoft Excel - Wor...   My Documents   3   7:57 PM

Target Market Definition

Based on the analysis information, you can now formulate your target market definition. In other words, based on the characteristics of the organizations that have purchased from you in the past, you can now determine the types of organizations that are most likely to buy from you in the future.

The results of an example analysis are shown below. Based on these results, your target market definition could read as follows: When selling widgets, organizations within the target market share the following characteristics:

- The types of businesses or industries include:
    - Utilities
    - Information
    - Finance and Insurance
    - Real Estate and Rental and Leasing

- The size of company is normally between 1 and 50 employees
- The company normally is already using a product from another supplier
- The company normally is also using gadgets in addition to widgets

B B SALES CONNECTIONS

Target Market Definition Analysis

Class of Characteristic	Characteristic	Customer Count	Sales Volume	Customer Count Percentage	Sales Volume Percentage
Type of Business	11 - Agriculture, Forestry, Fishing, and Hunting	0	$ -		
	21 - Mining	0	$ -		
	22 - Utilities	2	$ 32,507.00	20%	29%
	23-Construction	0	$ -		
	31 to 33 - Manufacturing	0	$ -		
	42 - Wholesale Trade	0	$ -		
	44 to 45 - Retail Trade	0	$ -		
	48 to 49 - Transportation and Warehousing	0	$ -		
	51 - Information	1	$ 5,678.00	10%	5%
	52 - Finance and Insurance	6	$ 39,043.00	60%	35%
	53 - Real Estate and Rental and Leasing	1	$ 34,509.00	10%	31%
	54 - Professional, Scientific and Technical Services	0	$ -		

Class of Characteristic	Characteristic	Customer Count	Sales Volume	Customer Count Percentage	Sales Volume Percentage
Number of Employees	Characteristic	Customer Count	Sales Volume	Customer Count Percentage	Sales Volume Percentage
	Unknown	0	$ -		
	1 – 4	2	$ 8,565.00	20%	8%
	5 – 9	4	$ 32,808.00	40%	29%
	10 – 19	2	$ 10,913.00	20%	10%
	20 – 49	2	$ 59,451.00	20%	53%
	50 – 99	0	$ -		
	100 – 249	0	$ -		
	250 – 499	0	$ -		
	500 – 999	0	$ -		
	1,000 – 4,999	0	$ -		
	5000 – 9,999	0	$ -		
	Over 10,000	0	$ -		
	0	0	$ -		

Class of Characteristic	Characteristic	Customer Count	Sales Volume	Customer Count Percentage	Sales Volume Percentage
Annual Revenue	Characteristic	Customer Count	Sales Volume	Customer Count Percentage	Sales Volume Percentage
	Unknown	3	$ 69,939.00	30%	63%
	Less than $500,000	3	$ 22,192.00	30%	20%
	$500,000 to $1 Million	3	$ 14,461.00	30%	13%
	$1 Million to $2.5 Million	1	$ 5,235.00	10%	5%
	$2.5 Million to $5.0 Million	0	$ -		

Class of Characteristic	Characteristic	Customer Count	Sales Volume	Customer Count Percentage	Sales Volume Percentage
Product Category Purchased	Characteristic	Customer Count	Sales Volume	Customer Count Percentage	Sales Volume Percentage
	Widget 1	3	$ 67,345.00	30%	60%
	Widget 2	4	$ 24,949.00	40%	22%
	Widget 3	2	$ 11,878.00	20%	11%
	Widget 4	1	$ 7,565.00	10%	7%
	Widget 5	0	$ -		

Class of Characteristic	Characteristic	Customer Count	Sales Volume	Customer Count Percentage	Sales Volume Percentage
Product Usage	Characteristic	Customer Count	Sales Volume	Customer Count Percentage	Sales Volume Percentage
	Low Volume	3	$ 12,878.00	30%	12%
	Medium Volume	5	$ 39,403.00	50%	35%
	High Volume	2	$ 59,451.00	20%	53%

Class of Characteristic	Characteristic	Customer Count	Sales Volume	Customer Count Percentage	Sales Volume Percentage
Previous Supplier	Characteristic	Customer Count	Sales Volume	Customer Count Percentage	Sales Volume Percentage
	Non User	2	$ 6,235.00	20%	6%
	Unknown Supplier	0	$ -		
	Competitor 1	5	$ 79,666.00	50%	71%
	Competitor 2	1	$ 10,488.00	10%	9%
	Competitor 3	1	$ 7,783.00	10%	7%
	Competitor 4	0	$ -		
	Competitor 5	1	$ 7,565.00	10%	7%

Class of Characteristic	Characteristic	Customer Count	Sales Volume	Customer Count Percentage	Sales Volume Percentage
Related Product	Characteristic	Customer Count	Sales Volume	Customer Count Percentage	Sales Volume Percentage
	None	1	$ 5,235.00	10%	5%
	Gadget 1	3	$ 25,836.00	30%	23%
	Gadget 2	4	$ 71,772.00	40%	64%
	Gadget 3	2	$ 8,894.00	20%	8%
	Gadget 4	0	$ -		

As you can see, the results can reveal some very interesting information. For example, sometimes the greatest number of customers in a certain category does not match the greatest dollar volume of sales. Such is the case with the "Type of Business" listing above. This is quite commonly referred to as the 80/20 rule. Loosely defined, it means that 80 percent of your outcomes are the result of 20 percent of your inputs, and vice versa. For our purposes, it means that 80 percent of your business comes from only 20 percent of your customers. It also means that 80 percent of your time is spent on customers that only bring in 20 percent of your business. Knowing this type of information is very important as you can then adjust your activities to spend more time on what makes you the most sales.

You will also note that not all of the classes of characteristics have been included in the target market definition. If the analysis does not show a clear trend in the data, it is best not to include it in your definition. Otherwise, your definition could become too narrow, and cause you to bypass sales opportunities. In our example, such is the case with Annual Revenue and Product Usage.

Sometimes you may want to be more specific in your analysis. This can be accomplished by doing more than one analysis, with a separate spreadsheet for each, and therefore creating more than one target market definition. For example, you could complete the analysis on just one product category at a time. Using the data from above, you could do your analysis on just Widget 1 alone, as opposed to Widget 1, 2, 3, 4 and 5 at the same time. In a separate version of the *Market Definition Worksheet.xls*, you would only list Widget 1 in your product category, and you would only input customers who had purchased Widget 1. The end result would be a more detailed target market definition for just Widget 1 alone, as opposed to all the products that you sell.

Regardless of how specific your definition, you now should have a very clear picture as to what defines your target market. In other words, you should now be able to easily describe your ideal prospect, therefore knowing where to concentrate your sales efforts to maximize your chances of making a sale. Nothing is guaranteed, but you want to ensure that you are focusing on where you are most likely to be successful!

WHAT IS A PROSPECT?

Now that we know the right organizations to target, it is just a matter of creating a prospect list and start calling, right? Not quite. If it were that simple, every sales representative would be at quota. It is true that you must start a sale before you can close it, and in order to do that, you first must make some sort of contact with a prospect. It is also true that now that your target market has been defined, you can now make a list of organizations to start making prospecting calls where you are more likely to find a prospect.

But what exactly is a prospect? What are the common characteristics that determine this company in your target market can buy and is therefore a sales opportunity today, versus another company in your target market that cannot buy and is not a sales opportunity today? The operative word that most sales representatives overlook is *today!*

There are four common characteristics that an organization within your target market must possess in order for them to be considered a prospect in B2B sales:

1. They must have an identified need or problem.
2. They must have the desire to satisfy that need or solve that problem.
3. They must have the ability to pay for the solution.
4. They must have a sense of urgency to act upon a solution immediately.

Regardless of your industry, every prospect must have these four characteristics. Think about the purchases you have made for yourself over the last while. In each and every case, you possessed all of four of these characteristics. For example, as a new B2B sales representative you may have the need for some sort of transportation so that you can visit your potential clients face to face. Walking to each customer may not be convenient, therefore your desire is to purchase a car as you feel this is the best solution to satisfy your needs. You must have the ability to pay for the car, since the dealership will not let you drive off the lot without a credit check and some sort of payment. Lastly, you know you must purchase the car immediately as it is, after all, a condition of your employment.

Stated quite simply, if one or more of the four characteristics listed above is missing, it must either be created by the sales process, or the prospect will not buy today. As they are in your target market, they may still buy from you, eventually, but they will not buy from you *today!*

When Do Your Prospects Buy?

Before we defined your target market, we stated that it was dangerous to assume that every business can buy from you. Just as it is dangerous to believe that, it is just as dangerous to believe that every business within your target market can buy from you at any time! For example, it is unlikely that you would lease a new car today when your current lease still has two years left. Therefore, before you start calling every company in your target market, you must define as to the time frame when the prospects within it can buy from you.

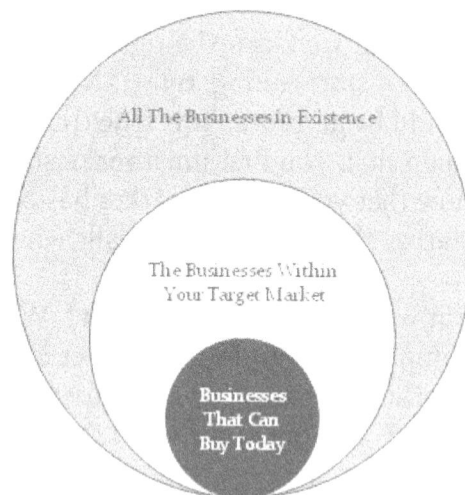

To do this, you must know how often a company buys or re-orders your product. Is it weekly, monthly, once every two to four years, or perhaps even once every five years or more? This is not to be confused with how often the company uses the product as this is quite different. What you need to know is how often they renegotiate the contract for the use of your product. For example, although most companies use a photocopier every day, they only tend to buy or renegotiate contracts for new copiers every three to five years. Or, although companies may make claims on their dental plans weekly, they only renegotiate the contract with their insurance carriers once a year.

Let's say that you know that there are a total of 10,000 companies in your sales territory. Let's also say that you have purchased a list from a mailing list broker, and you know that 2000 of these companies are within your defined target market. Lastly, let's say that you know that companies on average buy your product once every five years. Working the numbers (2000 companies divided by 5 years), you can calculate that only 400 companies within your target market are able to buy this year. The question is do you know which 400 companies they are? This is extremely important because if you are in the wrong place at the wrong time, the sales opportunity with any given company will not occur again for another five years!

As you can see, knowing how often a company can buy your product determines the timing of your sales opportunity. When you know this information, you can prescreen companies in your target market as you are prospecting them. In other words, you already know they are a prospect because they are in your target market. But now you will know if they are a prospect *today*. And if they are not a prospect today, you will be able to determine when they will be.

The Follow-Up File

The Follow-Up File is a tool for you to use to track information about each and every company that you prospect. However, it will not be organized alphabetically like the telephone book, but organized by the date of their next purchase based on the information that you gather when prospecting. Stated simply, the Follow-Up File increases your chances of being in the right place at the right time!

In the previous example, 400 of the 2000 or one in five companies in your target market were buying this year. If one in five prospects are buying this year, tracking the other four prospects as to when they are able to buy maximizes your valuable sales time, resources, and commissions!

The information contained in your Follow-Up File needs to be gathered in a very structured and organized fashion. Therefore, before you start to contact all the companies in your target market, you must determine what information you need to gather, and how it needs to be organized.

First, you should track the public information like company name, address, phone and fax number. You should also track key contacts within the organization, as well as their contact information such as their email address. Depending on your product, you may need to gather information on more than one key contact within the same organization.

All of the fields in your target market definition should also be tracked for each company prospected. For example, each company prospected should be classified using the lists that you created earlier for type of business, number of employees, annual revenue, product categories, product usage, competitive suppliers, and related products. By tracking information this way, you will be able to determine if the organization that you contacted is indeed in your target market as you suspected it was in the first place.

Lastly, and perhaps most importantly, you must track where your prospect is in the buying cycle. For example, if you know that companies tend to renegotiate contracts for your product every so many years, you need to track when each prospect last negotiated their current contract. By doing so, you can determine when they are most likely to negotiate the next one. In other words, you have determined if they are a prospect *today*. If the timing of the buying cycle is not right and therefore the company is not a prospect today, the information gathered will tell when they will be, and therefore when you should re-contact the company to open the sales process. This is the date by which the company should be filed in your Follow-Up file.

For example, if your prospects tend to renegotiate their contract every four years, and you contacted a company that renegotiated their current contract three and a half years ago, chances are that you have an excellent prospect for today as they will be signing a new contract within the next six months. On the other hand, if a company you contacted just renewed their contract last year, chances are that they will not be a prospect for another two and a half years, and therefore should be re-contacted then.

It is critical that each company in your Follow-Up File is filed by your next sales contact date. When you do so, the end result is that you have created a list of companies in your target market that is organized by the date of their next product purchase. Most sales representatives would consider this information a license to print their own commission cheques! If you don't do this, and just file each company alphabetically, all you have really done is create a glorified phone book!

Types of Follow-Up File Systems

A Follow-Up File system can either be a manual or an automated system, depending on the types of products sold, the user's preference and their level of computer skills. Both types of systems can be effective, as long as the system is set up correctly.

A manual system can be as simple as marking down your next contact date for each company in your calendar. Each day, the files for the companies listed on that day's calendar are retrieved and the company is contacted. Once the call is complete, the company file is returned to storage and the next sales contact date is entered into the calendar. This type of manual system can work very well if there are very few companies to be contacted in any given day. Otherwise, a lot of time, time that could be better spent selling, is spent filing and refilling company records.

Another type of a manual Follow-Up File system includes twelve file folders, one labeled for each month of the year. The information on each company that is gathered while prospecting is entered onto a single sheet. Once the next sales contact date is determined for a company, that single sheet is then filed in the corresponding month's file. At the start of each month, the file containing all of the month's follow up sheets is reorganized by the specific contact dates within the month. As the sales follow up calls are completed each day, the sheets are re-filed by the next contact date in the appropriate monthly folder.

This system can be extremely effective to ensure that you are contacting your prospects when they are most likely to buy. However, sometimes a previously contacted company will call you. If the company sheet is filed in a different month than the month you are working in, you may waste a lot of time searching through your monthly files to find the company information that you need. Also, as time goes on, this Follow-Up File will grow to contain numerous company information sheets. As this happens, again, you may start to spend too much valuable sales time re-filing.

If too much time is being spent administering a manual Follow-Up File, then it is recommended to automate your system. If automating can save enough time so that you can do just one more call per day, it is worth the investment. After all, just one more call a day is 240 calls per year. For some, that is like a whole extra month of work per year!

Also known as Customer Relationship Management (CRM) or database management systems, there are many inexpensive and easy to use software programs available on the market today. Maximizer™, Goldmine™, Act™, Outlook™, Access™, or even your employer's own internal program can all function as effective Follow-Up Files.

Choosing a software program to use as your Follow-Up File is largely a function of preference and budget, however it should have the following abilities:

- The ability to add user-defined fields. This will allow you to customize your Follow-Up File database to track your defined target market characteristics.
- The ability to customize drop down lists within these user-defined fields so that you could just choose the data being entered as opposed to having to type it in for each record. This ability drastically speeds data entry.
- The ability to add a "Next Sales Contact Date" field as a mandatory date field. In other words, you must add a date in the field, and it must be in the future, or the program will not accept it.
- The ability to sort the database by the "Next Sales Contact Date" field so that you can print a daily call sheet of your hot prospects.

Regardless of the type of Follow-Up File system that you choose, it is important that you *use* a Follow-Up File system, and that it be organized by the next contact date. In fact, it is critical for your success in sales!

Here is a true case in point. Over the course of a year, a local branch manager had seven separate photocopier sales people do face to face prospecting calls on her business. However, since the current equipment was on a lease with an expiry date far into the future, it was not the right time in the buying cycle for the company to be considered a prospect today. The branch manager asked each of the sales representatives to call back on the same specified date in the future. Of the seven representatives given this information on the timing of the next sale, only two called back! Only two!

Although this case may seem unbelievable, unfortunately, it is more the rule, as opposed to the exception. In fact, research shows that 2 out of 3 sales are made to customers who have said no not once, but 5 times! It also shows that 63% of sales are made after the 5th rejection. Wasted opportunities like the example above stem from the fact that 75% of all sales people give up after the 1st or 2nd rejection. Given this, it certainly is easy to see why 25% of all sales representatives produce 90-95% of all sales! These are the representatives who use a Follow-Up File system and don't give up too early!

The Keys to Successful Follow-Up Files

The following keys to success apply for both manual and automated Follow-Up File systems:

- When filing each company by the next sales contact date, use specific dates. For example, October 14 is preferred over just the month of October. This will allow you to spread your follow up calls throughout the month, making for better time management. Also, if everything is left until month end, not only is this a bad time to contact some prospects, but also all the calls may not get completed on time. A sales opportunity may get missed.

- Every company that you contact should be entered into your Follow-Up File system, even if it turns out that they are not a prospect today or in the future. Not only is it important for you to know where to go when, but is also important for you to know where not to go. By tracking this, you are less likely to spend you valuable sales resources contacting a company that you have already determined will never be a prospect.

- Enter the information for each company the exact same way. Commonalities across companies will become more apparent more quickly. Also, if using an automated system, this will make searching your database much easier and more accurate.

- Use only one system for both current and prospective customers. Tracking just your current customers only works if you have 100 per cent market share and you never again need to attract new customers. Since that is highly unlikely, you must also track your potential customers. Administering a separate system for each just wastes time and energy when in reality, the only reason for a Follow-Up File is to ensure that you are spending your sales resources on the company who is going to buy next, not just who has bought in the past. If it is important to know if a company is a current customer or not, then track it as a separate field in your Follow-Up File, as opposed to wasting time with two systems.

- Administering a Follow-Up File requires a daily commitment. It must be updated each and every day, no ifs, ands or buts! Simply don't leave the office until you have filed each call you made that day by the date of your next contact. If you follow up file says call today, call today! It is very impressive to a prospect for you to do exactly what you said you were going to do, when you said you were going to do it! Don't put off until tomorrow what can be done today!

THE PROSPECTING CALL

You have now defined your target market and you have determined which types of companies to contact. You have created your Follow-Up file and you have determined what information to track. The next step is to plan your prospecting approach that you will use with each company contacted.

The first step to any sale is the prospecting call. This includes any type of customer contact that attempts to initiate the sales process. This could be completed in many different ways, from telemarketing, to face to face contact, to the customer contacting you from the phone book.

Whether you are knocking on a door, telemarketing, or about to send an introductory email to another social network contact, if you do not plan your prospecting approach properly, you are only wasting your and the prospect's time. More specifically, you need to script exactly what you will say to each contact to ensure you are working with the right prospect at the right time.

Components of an Effective Prospecting Call

After completing Section 1, you have calculated that you need to do a certain number of prospecting calls each and every day in order for you to reach your income goals. Perhaps your activity tracking has shown that you need to do 20 prospecting calls a day to reach your goal. But what if your got better at how you prospect? What if you improved your skills and now you only have to do 15?

Regardless of your prospecting method, you can increase your effectiveness by ensuring that your prospecting calls include certain key components. When included, more of your prospecting calls will be successful, with success being defined as you and your prospective customer agreeing to proceed to the next step in the sales process, namely the fact find or information gathering stage.

Opening Greeting

The first element of an effective prospecting call is the opening greeting. The purpose of your opening greeting is to determine who is your key contact, and if possible, to speak with them. Whether you are prospecting face to face or on the telephone, most times this is completed with the receptionist.

Receptionists are very valuable contacts as they tend to know who does what in the organization better than anyone else. They are also responsible for greeting and assisting those that call the company, and therefore should be willing to answer your questions. However they can also be extremely busy people, often doing many tasks at the same time. As such, it is often more effective to respect their time and keep your opening greeting short and straight to the point.

If you have prospected the company before, you may already know the name of your key contact. If so, your opening greeting should be as simple as:
- "May I speak to John Doe, please."

However, if this is your first prospecting call on a company, you may not know who your key contact is yet. Or, if the name that you have was from some time ago, it would be a good idea to confirm the name you have is still your key contact. People change jobs regularly. Therefore the name that you received three months ago may not still be your key contact today.

A very effective opening greeting to use in these types of situations is:
- "Hi, I hope you can help me today. I am looking for the name of the person in charge of purchasing widgets."

As stated earlier, receptionists are responsible for greeting and assisting. The chance of any receptionist saying "no" to your request for help in the first sentence is extremely remote. If they did not want to help, they would not be receptionists in the first place!

Please note that the opening greeting specifically asks for the *name* of the person in charge, as opposed to just asking to *speak* to the person in charge. If you just ask to speak to the person and they are not available, your call could end without you gathering any more information than you had before you made the call. All you have done is waste your time.

By asking specifically for the name of the person, no matter what happens in the rest of the call, at least you have gathered the name of your key contact. In case they are not available, at least you have their name for next time. This alone makes your prospecting effort worthwhile!

Lastly, the title or responsibility of the person whose name you ask for is very dependent on the product or service that you sell. If you sell accounting software, you may ask for the name of the person in charge of purchasing for the finance or IT department. If you are selling packaging supplies, you may want to ask for the person in charge of purchasing for the shipping or facilities department.

Please note that you are asking for the person in charge of *purchasing* your product. If you do not actually use the word purchasing, often you will receive the name of the person who operates your product as opposed to the name of the person responsible for buying it. Operators and users are important in some buying decisions, but they rarely have the authority to make the final buying decisions. Those decisions are normally made by someone higher in the organization, someone who has budget accountabilities for the expense of the use of your product.

Although you are asking for the person in charge of *purchasing* your product, you are not actually asking for someone specifically in the purchasing department. A purchaser's role is to execute a purchase for a product based on another department's purchasing criteria. You key contact is actually the person in that other department.

For example, if you are sell group dental insurance, you may receive a purchase order from the purchasing department for your dental plan, but it was actually the Human Resources manager who decided the best dental plan to buy. Although a good contact to have, unless you sell actual purchase order forms, the name of a purchaser is not your ultimate contact.

If you are unsure as to whom you should ask for when you are prospecting, your sales manager and other sales representatives within your company can help. As a general rule, always ask for the person higher up in the organization. It is easier for a manager to refer you to a subordinate than it is for a subordinate to refer you to a manager. In other words, when in doubt, start at the top!

A Headline That Generates Interest

When people read the newspaper, it is very rare that they read every line of every article. There are just far too many articles and too little time! In reality, people only have enough time to scan the paper, reading only the articles where the headline has caught their interest.

Similarly, it is rare for key contacts to meet with every sales representative that calls. There are just far too many sales representatives and too little time! In reality, they will only invest their valuable time to meet with those representatives whose headline has caught their interest. When a prospect tells you, "I am not interested", what they really are telling you is that you were not interesting enough!

Just stating the product or service that you sell does not generate interest, but stating why it should be bought will. Why do your customers buy from you? What benefits do they realize by using your product or service? What makes you different from your competition? Quite simply, your headline must answer the question that is on every key contact's mind – "What is in it for me?"

For example, the statement, "My name is Sam Sales Rep, and I sell advertising for the Daily Press." is not a headline that would generate much interest. A headline that would generate more interest would be the statement like, "My name is Sam Sales Rep with the Daily Press. We have been able to help many businesses like yours acquire new customers and increase sales through the effective use of print advertising."

An effective headline can take some time to create. Ask your sales manager and other sales representatives within your company for their ideas on what headlines have worked for them. Review your company's advertising and brochures to see what headlines your marketing department believes are effective. Pay attention to what headlines grab your attention when you see or hear an advertisement.

Most effective headlines evolve over time. Nothing is cast in stone. You can always change your headline if needed. As you monitor your sales activity as described in Section 1, you will be able to see if your new headline is more effective than your old one. Just remember, an effective headline just needs to answer the question that your key contact is always asking - "What is in it for me?"

Qualifying Questions

The purpose of asking qualifying questions in your prospecting call is to determine if you are spending your valuable sales resources with the right company, at the right time. Specifically, the questions that you ask need to answer the following questions:

1. Is this company actually a prospect?
2. If yes, are they a prospect *today?*
3. If not today, then when?

Even if the key contact is not available, you could still ask the receptionist your qualifying questions. You may not get all the answers that you need, but you may get enough information to help you determine if the company is a prospect and whether you should invest further sales resources to touch base with the key contact or not.

The process of developing qualifying questions begins with your target market definition. More specifically, you should develop a question for each field that you will track in your Follow-Up File.

Some examples of qualifying questions to determine if the company is a prospect include:

- How many people are employed by your company?
- Do you currently use widgets?
- Who supplies your widgets?
- How many widgets do you use on a monthly basis?
- Many users of widgets also tend to use gadgets. Do you as well?

As stated earlier, you must also determine if the company is a prospect *today*. This is accomplished by asking a question in regards to the timing of the prospect's next purchase. Examples of questions to do this are as follows:

- How long have you been dealing with your current supplier?
- When did you last negotiate you current contact for widgets?

Agreement to Move to Next Step

Once you have received answers to your qualifying questions, you should be able to determine if the company you have contacted is indeed a prospect. If they are not, thank the prospect for his time, and end the call. If they are not a prospect, there is no point to proceed further. You should still track the information in your Follow-Up File, however, so that you do not waste sales resources trying to sell to them again in the future.

Similarly, if the answers that you receive tell you that the prospect will not be buying for some time, confirm a follow up date with the prospect, and then end the call. In other words, if your questions have told you that your prospect could buy from you, but they just cannot buy from you today, there is no point in continuing at this time. File the company in your Follow-Up File by the date of their next purchase and move on to your next potential prospect.

If the answers to your qualifying questions tell you that you are dealing with an actual prospect *and* that they are able to purchase from you in the near future, you should then proceed to obtain agreement from your prospect to move to the next step in your sales process, namely the fact finding stage.

- "John Doe, based on the information that you have given me, I believe that the use of our widgets could help you acquire new customers and increase revenues. The next step is for us to meet and for me to learn more about your company. Are you available on Tuesday at 10:00 am, or do you prefer Wednesday at 2:00 pm?"

When asking the prospect for an appointment for the fact find, the question should be worded as to give the prospect a choice between two alternative meeting times. This forces the prospect to choose between the two options given. By just offering one possible meeting time, the prospect could just say "no" to the meeting all together.

Your Final Prospecting Script

Now that you know the elements of an effective prospecting call, you can actually develop a script to include them and increase your success rate. Your final script will depend on your industry, and the product or service that you sell. It is important to plan your script ahead of time so that it includes all the elements of an effective prospecting call.

It is suggested that you write your script out, including your opening statement, your headline, all of your qualifying questions and your agreement to move to the next step statements. You should also rehearse your script. The more you practice it, the more comfortable you will be using it. You will also be less likely to miss important information that may help you determine if you are dealing with an actual prospect, and if they are a prospect *today*. Bottom line, the more preparation work that you do, the more effective your prospecting will be.

On the next page is an example of a prospecting call, from the opening statement to the agreement to move to the next step. It includes the different possible outcomes that may occur, depending on the answers that you receive from your prospect.

B B SALES *CONNECTIONS*

Sample Telemarketing Approach

Opening Statement
Sales Rep - Hi, I hope you can help me. I am looking for the name of the person in charge of purchasing Widgets.
Receptionist - That would be John Doe
Sales Rep - Is John Doe available?

Headline	Headline
Receptionist - One moment please. John Doe - Hi, John Doe speaking. Hi John. My name is Sam Sales Rep of ABC company. Many companies similar to yours have, after using our widgets, that they have aquired new customers and increased revenues.	Receptionist - No, I'm sorry. He is out of the office today. My name is Sam Sales Rep of ABC company. Many companies similar to yours have, after using our widgets, that they have aquired new customers and increased revenues.

Qualifying Questions	Qualifying Questions
Sales Rep - How many people are employed by your company? Sales Rep - Does your company currently use widgets? Sales Rep - Who supplies your widgets? Sales Rep - How many widgets do you use on a monthly basis? Sales Rep - Many users of widgets also tend to use gadgets. Do you as well? Sales Rep - When did you last negotiate your widget supplier?	Sales Rep - How many people are employed by your company? Sales Rep - Does your company currently use widgets? Sales Rep - Who supplies your widgets? Sales Rep - How many widgets do you use on a monthly basis? Sales Rep - Many users of widgets also tend to use gadgets. Do you as well? Sales Rep - How long have you been using your widget supplier?

Agreement to Move To Next Step	Agreement to Move To Next Step	Agreement to Move To Next Step	Agreement to Move To Next Step	Agreement to Move To Next Step
Sales Rep - John Doe, based on the information that you have given me, I believe that the use of our widgets could help you acquire new customers and increase revenues. The next step is for us to meet and for me to learn more about your company. Are you available on Tuesday at 10:00 am, or do you prefer Wednesday at 2:00 pm?	Sales Rep - John Doe, based on the information that you have given me, I believe that the use of our widgets could help you acquire new customers and increase revenues, however not at this time. As you will be renegotiating your widget contract next year, I would like to call you back in 10 months time. Does this time frame work for	Sales Rep - John, based on the information that you have given me, I do not believe that I can help your company at this time. Here is my contact information. Please feel free to contact me should we be able to be of service in the future.	Sales Rep - Thank you very much for your time. I think that I can help your company. I will call back and speak to John Doe. When is the best time to reach him?	Sales Rep - Thank you very much for your time. I do not believe that I can help your company at this time. Here is my contact information for John Doe. Please let him know for him to contact me should we be able to be of service in the future.
John Doe - Tuesday at 10 works best for me. Sales Rep - I look forward to our meeting. See you	John Doe - That sounds about right. Sales Rep - Great! I will talk to you then. Thanks	John Doe - Thanks. I will keep you number on file Sales Rep - Thanks for your time.	Receptionist - Normally first thing in the morning. Sales rep - Thanks very much for your help.	Receptionist - No problem. Sales Rep - Thanks very much for your help.

On the next page is the *Prospecting Approach Worksheet.xls* that you can use to script your prospecting calls. It will help you to ensure that your script includes all the elements of an effective prospecting call, therefore maximizing your chance of success.

B2B SALES CONNECTIONS

Prospecting Approach Worksheet

Enter information in yellow boxes to script your prospecting approach.

Step 1 - Opening Statement

Hi, I hope you can help me. I am looking for the name of the person in charge of

Step 2 - Headline

Hi, my name is _____ of _____ company.

We've been able to help companies similar to yours

Step 3 - Qualifying Questions

Qualifing Question #1

Qualifing Question #2

Qualifing Question #3

Qualifing Question #4

Qualifing Question #5

Time Frame Question #1

Time Frame Question #2

Step 4 - Agreement to Move To Next Step Statement

Based on the information that you have provided, I believe that I can help you

The next step is

Are you available on _____ or do you prefer

Thank you very much for your time.

WHERE TO FIND PROSPECTS TO CONTACT

All the preparation is complete! By defining your target market, you have determined which type of companies to contact. By creating your Follow-Up file and prospecting approach, you have determined what questions to ask and how to track the information received when you contact them. The next step is to actually start contacting these companies and start the sales process!

It is best if you work from some sort of list when prospecting. That way you can call company after company, without wasting time trying to figure out whom to contact next. Creating a prospecting list can be quite simple and you will find the information you need is readily available from several different sources.

Business Directories

A business directory is simply a list of companies. They are readily available and are probably the most widely used source for creating prospecting lists for business to business sales.   Some directories only include the company name and contact information, while others also include detailed descriptions like the number of employees, annual revenues and the industry in which they operate.

The more information that is included in the directory, the easier it will be to identify those companies who are in your target market as you defined it earlier. Taken a step further, the easier it is to identify your target companies, the more effective your prospecting efforts will be. You will waste less time contacting companies that are very unlikely to buy, and spend more time with those that will. In other words, you will be working smarter, not harder.

The most common business directory available is your local yellow pages, however most sales representatives find more detailed directories at their local library, either in a book or electronic file format. Your municipal government may also have a directory available, as do many local business associations such as your Chamber of Commerce or Board of Trade.

Lastly, a simple internet search will also yield many online directories, many of which can be viewed on the internet at no charge or downloaded for a nominal fee. You can also use data capture software like ListGrabber from www.egrabber.com to build your prospect lists from free lead sources and databases found on the Internet.

List Brokers

A list broker is essentially a service that sells prospect lists created from their own managed business directories. The difference from the directories discussed earlier is that a list broker can segment the directory so you only purchase listings of companies that you know are in your target market. For example, you can only buy listings for companies that are a certain size or operate in certain industries.

Although lists purchased from list brokers tend to be more expensive than a general business directory, the benefits of starting with a detailed and targeted list may make the investment worthwhile.

Online Social Networks

There can be no mistake that online social networking has exploded in the past few years. Almost every person and every business has an online profile these days, and if they don't now, chances are they will soon.

Generally speaking, the three main social networking websites are Facebook (www.facebook.com), Twitter (www.twitter.com) and LinkedIn (www.linkedin.com). Although many people are using all three networks to generate sales leads effectively, the main site for business networking seems to be LinkedIn. On LinkedIn, you can perform searches by company, job title, industry and geographic location, therefore creating very targeted lists for prospecting.

Regardless of the site, every user maintains and updates their own profile information. Therefore, the real advantage to sales people is that social networks are essentially the most current and most accurate prospecting lists available. However the danger is, if not managed properly, social networks are only glorified phone books that end up being huge time wasters for those who use them.

To prevent this from occurring, no matter where you are social networking, you must segment your contacts into categories so you can target your efforts as described earlier. Facebook, Twitter and LinkedIn all give you the ability to do this with their built in features. Take the time to create your own personalized lists or tags, and then classify every contact you have within them. To help you build and maintain relationships with each of your contacts, you can use an online social networking contact management system like Network Hippo from networkhippo.com.

Geographical Prospecting

Geographical prospecting is essentially picking a certain area, perhaps a street or postal code, and knocking on each door looking to make contacts. While some sales people consider this to be too "old school", it can still be an effective way to create prospecting lists to contact later by telephone.

The key is door to door prospecting is to ensure that instead of just dropping off business cards, you are qualifying each prospect using the prospecting approach you developed earlier. It is also important to maintain your follow up file system to ensure if they are not a prospect today, you will contact them when they will be.

HOW OFTEN TO CONTACT A PROSPECT

Even if your prospect is smack dab in the middle of the bull's eye of your target market, chances are you will not open the sales process on your very first contact. In fact, studies have shown that two out of three sales are made to prospects who have said "no" not once, but five times! Another study stated that someone will have to hear your company name at least three times before it will even register enough for him to remember it. One very successful sales rep stated he must leave an average of seven to ten voice mails before his messages are returned.

When all is said and done, a customer will buy on his time line, not yours. If he will not buy today, you must develop a plan to stay in touch with him so that when he is ready to buy, he will think of you first.

As discussed previously, it is critical that each company in your Follow-Up File be filed by your next sales contact date. This is determined by your customer's buying cycle. For example, if your prospects tend to renegotiate their contract every four years, and you contacted a company that renegotiated their current contract three and a half years ago, chances are that you have an excellent prospect for today as they will be signing a new contract within the next six months.

On the other hand, if a company just renewed their contract last year, chances are that they will not be a prospect for another two and a half years, and therefore should be re-contacted at that time to begin the sales process. In the meantime, you should stay in contact with that prospect so when it is time to start the sales process, the customer will do so very willingly.

What is the best method of staying in touch? You could send a letter or call the prospect to share some business news he may find interesting. You could automate the contact process by using an email service to regularly send a newsletter or you could make an introduction to another one of your contacts on your social network. The point is to stay in frequent contact so you start to build a relationship with the prospect. It's like every contact is a drip of water. On its own, it doesn't amount to much, but over time, each drip can add up to a very large pool!

As a sales representative, one of the biggest benefits of regular contact is it can eliminate surprises when it comes time to start the sales process. For example, it is common for people to move or to change jobs. If you stay in touch, you will already know the new contact's name and will have started to build a relationship with them ahead of time, therefore increasing your chances of making the sale.

How often you contact your prospects with your "drip" marketing campaign will depend on your product and the average prospect's buying cycle, however there are some general guidelines you should keep in mind:

- If the buying cycle of the prospect indicates he will purchase your product within the next six months, the frequency of contact should be at least once per month until you obtain the fact find appointment
- If you believe the prospect will purchase in the next year, the minimum frequency should be once per quarter, moving to once per month in the last six months before the purchase
- When the prospect is not likely to buy for a few years to come, you should contact them at least once per year, and then increase the frequency as time goes by.
- If you are not sure of the customer's buying cycle, or you sell the type of product that can be purchased at any time when the prospect may see fit, contact should be made at least once per quarter until you determine otherwise

As stated earlier, you want to stay in touch with your prospects so that when they are ready to buy your product or service, you are top of mind. Therefore, you really can't stay in touch too often. When in doubt, make the follow- up call!

CONCLUSION

After completing Section 1 of the Sales Training Course, you had calculated how many prospecting calls per day you need to complete to reach your income goals. Perhaps your number was 20 prospecting calls a day. Now, after completing this section, you will be better at how you prospect. By defining your target market, administering your Follow-Up File and honing your prospecting approach, perhaps you will only have to 15 calls instead of 20.

Now take that a step further. What if you still do the 20? Can you imagine how much you would surpass your goals?

Not doing more than average is what keeps the average down." – William M. Winans

APPENDIX – MANUAL CALCULATION FORMS

For those of you who are not familiar with Excel spreadsheets, all the calculations discussed in this training module can also be done manually. Simply print the forms on the following pages and follow the instructions.

Excel is a very common business software program. It is highly recommended that you take the time to learn the basics. Not only will you find that it can make your life much easier, you will find it to be a very profitable business tool as well.

B2B SALES CONNECTIONS

Target Market Characteristic Definitions

Number	Type of Business Listing	Number of Employees Listing	Annual Revenue Listing	Product Category Purchased Listing	Product Usage Listing	Previous Supplier Listing	Related Product Listing	Other Commonality Listing #1	Other Commonality Listing #2
1									
2									
3									
4									
5									
6									
7									
8									
9									
10									
11									
12									
13									
14									
15									
16									
17									
18									
19									
20									
21									
22									
23									
24									
25									
26									
27									
28									
29									
30									
31									
32									
33									
34									
35									
36									
37									
38									
39									
40									
41									
42									
43									
44									
45									
46									
47									
48									
49									
50									

B·B SALES CONNECTIONS

Target Market Definition Worksheet

Customer Name	Volume of Sale	Type of Business	Number of Employees	Annual Revenue	Product Category Purchased	Product Usage	Previous Supplier	Related Product	Other Commonality #1	Other Commonality #2

B₂B SALES CONNECTIONS

Target Market Definition Analysis

Class Of Characteristic	Characteristic	Customer Count	Sales Volume	Customer Count Percentage	Sales Volume Percentage
	Totals				

Chapter 3 - Why Do Prospects Buy? The Fact Find

"I have more fun and enjoy more financial success
when I stop trying to get what I want and start
helping other people get what they want."
– Spencer Johnson & Larry Wilson

WHY DO PROSPECTS BUY?

One of the most valuable lessons that you can learn as a sales representative is that prospects buy for their own reasons, not yours. Everyone that is involved in a purchasing decision is always thinking "What is in it for me?" If you can help your prospects get to where they want to go, or help them to accomplish what it is that they want to accomplish, you will be very successful in B2B sales.

Why Do Businesses Buy

What does a business want to accomplish? It is quite simple, really. The ultimate goal of any business is to make a profit. Even a non-profit organization must generate enough profit to cover expenses and still do the work in its mandate. The only way for a business to reach this goal is to generate more revenue than it spends on expenses. The balance remaining is the company's profit. Therefore basic math tells us that to increase profit, an organization has to either increase revenue or decrease expenses.

You may be thinking that the products you sell are too insignificant to affect a company's bottom line, but that is not the case. Absolutely everything a company buys affects its bottom line. Even a pencil that lasts longer, or is less expensive than the previous one purchased helps a company to make more profit.

In fact, there are many ways that your products or service can positively affect an organization's profit:

- Provide the same product or service the company is already using for less money than they are currently paying.
- Provide a better product or service for the same money than the company is currently spending.

- Provide a product or service that helps the company acquire new customers or sell more to existing customers.
- Provide a product or service that saves time or improves employee productivity.

Given that the ultimate goal is to make a profit, any product or service that you are selling must be perceived as helping your customer to make more profit, either by increasing revenue or by reducing expenses.

Why Do People Buy

Although businesses buy for profit, the people that work for those businesses buy for their own personal reasons. This does not mean that people are unethical, or that they are not acting in their company's best interest. It just means that when making purchasing decisions for their companies, people cannot simply turn off their own personal needs and biases.

For example, if someone makes a great purchasing decision that substantially increases the company's profit, that person may earn a promotion. Or if another person makes a purchasing decision that improves employee productivity and therefore improves the company's bottom line, that person may just be content that they now can make it home to have dinner with the family every night. Yet another person might make a purchasing decision based solely on the fact that he does not have to hear his staff complain any more.

To complicate things, sometimes several people are involved in the same corporate purchasing decision, each with their own personal needs and biases. Sometimes these needs can be aligned with each other, and sometimes they can conflict. More importantly, each person will view the benefits of your product differently, and therefore will evaluate your product differently.

People who make purchasing decisions for their companies are human. Whether they choose to admit it or not, part of those purchasing decisions are based on their own self interests. As such, in order to be successful in business to business sales, you must not only be able to identify how your product will help your prospect's company succeed, but you also must be able to position your product or service so that it helps the buyer satisfy his own self interests.

Your Prospect's Perception is Your Reality

Prospects buy products based on the perceived value they will derive from those products. However, what one prospect values is not the same as another. They both may buy the same product, but they can buy it for completely different reasons.

For example, why do people buy cotton swabs? Whatever answer came to your mind is the correct answer, but it is only the correct answer for you. Fashion models may see these products as cosmetic applicators, whereas parents may see them as ear cleaners for their children. A computer repair technician could see cotton swabs as keyboard cleaners, whereas a car repair shop could see them as touch up paint applicators.

More importantly, not only do people use cotton swabs differently, but they would also look for different features when choosing among the different brands. For example, the computer technician might consider a strong shaft important so it won't bend when pushing it in between the keyboard keys. A parent, on the other hand, might consider this same feature dangerous when cleaning a baby's ears, and as a result, may choose the swab with the fluffiest tip. The car repair shop and the fashion model however, may not want a fluffy tip which could leave lint in the finished product.

The point is that no two people are the same, and therefore no two people will perceive the value of your products the same. Because customers use your products differently, and because they have different self-interests, they place a different value on the same item. As business to business sales professionals, we must accept the fact that our customer's perception of our product's value is the reality in which we operate. We simply cannot use the same sales approach with every prospect.

Why Prospects Don't Buy

Most prospects think they are happy with their current way of doing things. They think that the status quo is working just fine and they don't see a need to change. If they did, they would have called you before you called them! If by some chance the prospect was unhappy enough that they actually picked up the phone to call you, they would have called your competitors as well.

You need to differentiate yourself or your prospect will simply not act, or worse, you will lose the sale to the lowest bidder. No matter what product you are selling, or how well trained you are to sell it, if the prospect does not perceive value in your solution, he will not buy it, no matter what the price!

Remember, everyone wants the cheapest price, but the cheapest price for what they want. And what the customer wants is the solution that has the highest perceived value. The only way to know what your prospect perceives is of value is to ask them in the fact find stage of the sales process.

THE FACT FIND

The fact find is the second step of the sales process. It is the result of the prospecting activities completed in step one. Simply put, any sales call that is intended to gather or confirm information about your prospective customer is considered a fact find.

Given the reasons that prospects buy, successful sales representatives consider the fact find the most important stage of the sales process. At this stage, you are gathering all the relevant information needed to prepare your offer to the customer. More importantly, this is where the prospect is going to tell you what he needs to buy, and why he is going to buy it.

Closing a sale is a natural evolution of the sales process. As such, the close actually starts here!

Objectives of the Fact Find

The main objective of a fact find is to gather all the information necessary to complete your presentation of offer to the customer. In other words, a fact find is considered successful if you and your prospect confirm that the sales process should continue to the last step of the sales process, that being the presentation of offer stage.

A complete and thorough fact find accomplishes the following:

- Identifies the relevant contacts within the organization.
- Identifies buying processes within the organization.
- Determines if sales opportunities actually exist.
- Identifies the time frames of those sales opportunities.
- Creates perceived value.
- Gathers all technical information required for system creation and design (if applicable for your product or service).
- Creates rapport and trust between you and the prospect.
- Obtains permission to continue to the presentation of offer stage.

A common mistake of sales representatives is to give the price too early in the buying cycle, before the fact find is truly completed. Then they wonder why the sale will not close after they have presented their proposal. Chances are that they did not really complete the fact find and therefore the customer does not perceive value in the proposed solution. The purpose of the fact find is to discover how, when and why the prospect will buy. Then, and only then, should you give a price!

Whom Should You Meet

Normally, your first fact interview will be with the same person who booked the appointment in the prospecting stage of the sales process. As discussed in Section 2, this should be the person who is in charge of *purchasing* your product. This is not someone specifically in the purchasing department, but the person who has budget accountabilities for the expense of your product. To complete your first fact find, the more senior the position within the organization, the better.

Often, the person in charge of purchasing will not know all the details of the necessary requirements for your product. Depending on the product or service that you are selling, the fact find may be completed in one meeting, or it may take several meetings with several different people.

For example if you are selling group dental plans, you may need to meet with the Human Resources manager to determine what the plan should cover, and the overall budget. You may also need to meet with the plan administrator to see if there are any issues with claims administration that need to be addressed. Ideally, you would want to meet with both of these parties together so that each can appreciate the others point of view, however that is not always possible.

Again, depending on your industry, a thorough needs analysis may require you to complete more than one fact find appointment at the same company. It is critical to your success that you do not take short cuts when completing this step of the sales process. If in doubt, complete another fact find!

Your Opening Greeting

When you completed your prospecting call and booked an appointment with the prospect, you set an expectation with your customer. You stated that you could help in some way, and that is why the prospect agreed to meet with you in the first place. As such, the opening greeting of your fact find must address that expectation and should remind them of why you agreed to meet.

Below is an example of an opening greeting for a fact find interview.

- "As I mentioned to you on the phone, I believe that the use of our widgets could help you to acquire new customers and increase revenues. Before I can tell you more about how I may be able to do that, I need to learn more about you and your company. To make the best use of our time, I have prepared a number of questions that will help us uncover the information that I need. May I proceed?"

As you can see, this relates directly back to the prospecting call script as discussed in Section 2. It reminds the customer of why he agreed to meet with you, and what benefit he will realize when he takes the time to answer your questions. It also makes the customer more open so he will give you the valuable information that you need. In other words, it answers the question that all potential customers are thinking, "what is in it for me?"

Create Your Questions

The keys to a successful fact find interview are the questions that you ask. They should be carefully pre-planned so that you will not leave the meeting only to discover that you forgot to obtain information that you will need later. They should also be scripted so that they guide you and the customer to logically discover his perceived value of your products.

Think of yourself as a lawyer asking questions of a witness on the witness stand. After careful and detailed preparation, the lawyer only asks specific questions, in a specific order. By doing this, the lawyer not only uncovers important information, but he also leads the witness to the conclusion that the lawyer desires. The same is true of a sales representative in a fact find.

To ensure that you are not leaving any stones unturned, the questions asked in a fact find should focus on the following:

- General company information
- Product and industry specific information
- Financial and buying process information

General Company Questions

General company information questions include company name, address, website, phone number, etc.. Most of this information can be found on a business card. I know this may seem very basic, but ensure that you always obtain a business card of everyone you meet in a prospect's organization. This will not only ensure that you spell the contact's name properly on your proposal, but also that you have the proper title.

When you receive a business card, give it a quick glance. If it does not have the person's email address on it, ask for it, since this is now the preferred method of communication in today's business world.

Other important general company information questions to ask include:

- Size of the company in terms of number of employees and/or annual revenues
- Other company offices including the location of the head office
- The type of business or the industry in which the prospect operates

You may already have this information from the research you completed before the fact find meeting, however it never hurts to confirm this information with your prospect in person.

Product & Industry Specific Questions

As stated earlier, everyone wants the cheapest price, but the cheapest price for what they want. The key is *the want.* A proper fact find actually helps to define and create that want so that you increase your chance of making the sale.

Have you ever heard someone say, "my machine works fine" or "I am happy with my current supplier"? I'll bet yes, and I'll bet on more than one occasion! It is not that the customer will not benefit from your product or service, he just does not yet *want* it. He does not yet know that there is more value to be realized from the use of your product. Your questions will allow him to discover that he can! A proper and complete fact find helps the customer to buy the right solution because it defines what the customer actually wants, not just what he thinks he wants.

To create your questions for the product and industry specific information, you first must know why your prospect might buy from you. What are the main benefits of using your product? What are your main advantages over your competition? What are the main problems the prospect may face by not using your product or service?

When you know this information, you can then develop questions so that you are creating the minimum requirements or "must haves" in the customer's mind. The customer will begin to think, "If I am going to buy widgets, my widgets must have this feature!" You will raise the customer's expectations of what he actually wants!

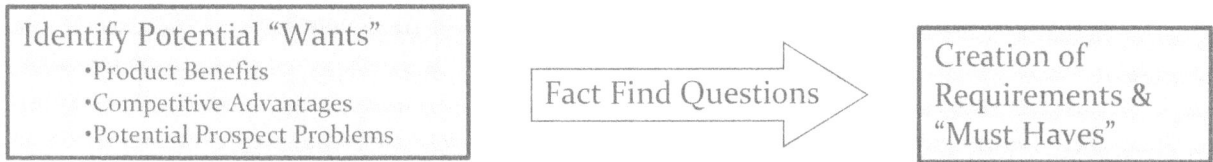

| Identify Potential "Wants"
•Product Benefits
•Competitive Advantages
•Potential Prospect Problems | Fact Find Questions ⟶ | Creation of Requirements & "Must Haves" |

As stated earlier, no two prospects are the same. Therefore, not all of your questions will yield new requirements. The key is to ask the questions so that you discover the "must haves" and create perceived value.

The actual questions that you ask in this section of the fact find will be dependent on your industry. However, below are some question formats that you can adapt to your product so that you build value in your prospects eyes.

- Product Benefit
  - Mr. Prospect, a feature that you current widget does not have is _____. Customers who have added this feature have told us that they realized the benefit of _____. Would this feature benefit you in the same way? How would it benefit you?

- Competitive Advantage
  - Mr. Prospect, some users of your brand of widgets have told us that they have experienced an issue with _____. Have you ever experienced this issue? How did that affect your operation? Would it help if we solved that issue? How would it help?

- Prospect Problem
  - Mr. Prospect, our customers have told us that when they started to use our widget, they experienced an increase (or decrease) in _____. Would this type of change also be of benefit to your organization? How would it help?

Notice that these questions started with the use of closed ended questions (can only be answered with a "yes" or "no"), and then moved to open ended or implication type questions. The closed ended question is like sending in a probe to see if there is a potential customer "must have" in this area. If you get a "yes" here, you continue with the implication questions to build the customer requirement.

Other product or industry specific questions to ask in the section of the fact find include:
- Product usage questions
  - o How many widgets do you use on a yearly basis?
  - o Has that increased from last year or stayed the same?
  - o Do you forecast that will increase or decrease next year?

- Related product questions
  - o Many companies who use widgets also use gadgets. Do you?

- Current supplier questions
  - o How long have you been using your brand of widgets?
  - o When did you last re-negotiate your contract with your current supplier?
  - o What do like about your current supplier?
  - o What could your current supplier do better?
  - o Who were you using before your current supplier?
  - o Why did you change?
  - o Has your current supplier met your expectations in terms of customer service? How so?

As you can see, these questions can be quite different depending on the product or service that you are selling, and the industry in which you operate. You may have many questions or just a few. They may be general in nature, or they may be very specific. Either way, it is highly recommended to write out your questions ahead of time and that you start with closed ended questions, and then move to open ended implication questions whenever possible.

Scripting your fact find this way will guarantee that you will gather all the information that you require. More importantly, you will ensure that you probe all of the potential "must haves" so that you can truly differentiate yourself from your competition. You will be perceived as the only supplier who meets the prospect's minimum requirements. If you are the only supplier who can do this, then you would automatically have the lowest price for what the customer wants.

Financial & Buying Process Questions

The last section of the fact find concerns the financial and buying process of your prospect's organization. In this section, you need to identify the key decision makers within the organization, as well as learn how and when your customer will buy.

Although gathering information on these subjects is critical to your success as a sales professional, many representatives do not feel comfortable asking these questions. They either fear that they are over stepping their bounds, that they will alienate the person they are meeting with, or that they are speaking on subjects that are above their business knowledge. Again, preparation and scripting can alleviate those insecurities. When you have planned and written out the questions, you will feel more confident when asking them.

Examples of questions on the financial and buying process of your prospects are listed below.

- What are the costs associated with how you are doing things now?
- What is the normal buying process in your company?
- Should anyone else join us when I return with my proposal? How do they fit into the decision making process?
- Besides yourself, who else in your organization would like to see a solution to this issue? Are they involved on the implementation side of the project, or do they also have budget accountabilities?
- Do you have budget set aside for this project in this year's or next year's budget? How much have you set aside?
- When is your fiscal year end?
- If our solution were to meet your needs, what is your timing for implementation?
- What are the three main criteria you will use to evaluate the proposed solutions?
- What specifically will happen when I return with my proposal?

As you can see, some of the questions are very similar. In fact, you may not need to ask each question listed, or you may need to go into more detail in other areas. Choose questions that are relevant to your industry and include them in your fact find questionnaire. As long as you discover who, how and when the customer buys, you have gathered enough information.

Your Closing Statement

When all is said and done, and the last question has been asked, you need to close the meeting. The best way to do this is to come full circle and relate this back to why the prospect agreed to meet with you in the first place.

Below are examples of closing statements for fact find interviews.

- "Thanks you for the information today. Based on our conversation, I believe that the use of our widgets can help you to acquire new customers and increase revenues. Before I can put my ideas on paper, I need more information on the day to day use of widgets in your organization. You mentioned earlier that Sam handles that side of this project. I would like to meet with Sam and then report back to you next week. Are you available Tuesday at 10:00 am, or do you prefer Wednesday at 2:00 pm?"

- "Thank you for the information today. Based on our conversation, I believe that the use of our widgets can help you to acquire new customers and increase revenues. I would like to go back to my office, put my ideas on paper, and then return next week to discuss them with you. Are you available Tuesday at 10:00 am, or do you prefer Wednesday at 2:00 pm?"

Notice how the last sentences keep the sales process moving forward. One of the biggest mistakes made by sales representatives is that they finish the fact find meeting with a statement like, "I'll get back to you when my proposal is ready." Weeks can go by before the next meeting, and by then all the momentum of creating the "must haves" has long since been forgotten.

A fact find is only considered successful if you and your prospect confirm that the sales process should continue to the next step, and when that will take place. Eliminate voice mail. Always book the next appointment.

Create Your Fact Find

On the next page is the *Fact Find Creation Worksheet.xls* that you can use to create your own fact find. Using it will help you to ask better questions, and maximize your chance of success.

B Sales Connections

Fact Find Creation
Worksheet

Enter information in the yellow boxes to create your fact find.

Step 1 - Opening Greeting

As I mentionned to you on the phone, I believe the use of our	
could help you	

Before I can tell you more about how I may be able to do that, I need to learn more about you and your company.

To make the best use of our time, I have prepared a number of questions that will help us uncover the information that I need. May I proceed?

Step 2 - General Company Questions

Question #1	
Question #2	
Question #3	
Question #4	
Question #5	

Step 3 - Product & Industry Specific Questions

Potential Want #1	
Questions	
Potential Want #2	
Questions	
Potential Want #3	
Questions	
Potential Want #4	
Questions	
Potential Want #5	
Questions	
Potential Want #6	
Questions	

Step 4 - Financial & Buying Process Questions

Question #1	
Question #2	
Question #3	
Question #4	
Question #5	

Step 5 - Agreement to Move To Next Step Statement

Based on the information that you have provided, I believe that I can help you			
The next step is			
Are you available on		or do you prefer	
Thank you very much for your time.			

CONCLUSION

People buy for their own reasons, not the sales representative's. Complicating this is the fact that everyone is different, and therefore everyone evaluates the perceived value of the products they purchase differently.

The most successful sales professionals know that the only way to truly help a customer buy is to ask the right questions.

The better the fact find, the happier the customer, the better the pay cheque!

Chapter 4 - Selling Your Solution
The Presentation of Offer

"Do not say a little in many words but
a great deal in a few." – Pythagoras

THE PRESENTATION OF OFFER

The final step in the sales process is the presentation of offer stage. This is where you are selling your solution! The fact find told you how, when and why the prospect will buy. The next logical step is for you to give him the information he needs so that he will buy.

Any sales call that presents or clarifies what you are selling is considered a presentation. This could include presenting a written proposal, or an equipment demonstration, or both. It could also include any call needed to answer any objections your customer may have, or any appointment needed to complete your sales order paperwork.

The exact form of the presentation of offer stage, and the number of calls required to complete it, will depend on your industry and the product or service that you are selling. However, regardless of your industry, the key to an effective presentation is to give the prospect just enough information so that he can make the buying decision. The old saying, "too much information" also applies in sales!

Objectives of the Presentation

The ultimate goal of a presentation is to get the sale. To achieve this, it is often necessary to achieve smaller objectives along the way. These include:

- Make your prospect comfortable to do business with you and your company.
- Present solutions to the problems uncovered in the fact find.
- Satisfy the "must haves" created in the fact find.
- Build your perceived value versus the status quo or the competition.
- Inform the prospect exactly how the solution will be implemented.
- Define the responsibilities of both the buyer and the seller when implementing the solution.
- Set the time frame for the sale.

As was just stated, the ultimate goal of a presentation is to get the sale. True, a presentation of offer sales call is successful if you and your prospect agree to proceed to close the sale by the customer ordering your product or service. However, just as important, is that when you close one sale, your presentation should also give you the opportunity to start another.

Whom Should You Meet

Your first presentation of offer appointment will be with the person you booked the appointment with in the fact find stage of the sales process. As discussed previously, this should be the person in charge of purchasing your product. This is not someone specifically in the purchasing department, but someone who has budget accountabilities for the expense of your product.

Sometimes, presentation meetings will be with a group of people, each having a different interest for purchasing or using your product. The identities and roles of each meeting attendee should have been identified in the fact find appointment beforehand. Even still, this should be confirmed very early in the presentation meeting. You need to know how everyone fits into the bigger picture.

Using a previous example, if you are selling group dental plans, you would be making your presentation to the Human Resources manager since this person decides on what the plan should cover, as well as its budget. It would not be uncommon for the Human Resources manager to also invite the plan administrator to this meeting to ensure that any issues with claims administration are addressed.

Depending on your industry, you may need to meet with several different people from several different departments before the final buying decision is made. This could include representatives from sales, finance, service, or IT. Be careful though. Too many people at one presentation can make for a very long and unproductive meeting. If this is the case, it may be best to arrange for a separate presentation meeting.

The more contacts you identify in the fact find, the better. Your sales manager or your colleagues will also be able to help you with exactly who factors into the buying decisions of your products. A good rule of thumb is that when in doubt always start at the top, and meet with the person as high up in the organization as possible.

TYPES OF PRESENTATIONS

As mentioned earlier, the presentation of offer stage of the sales process includes any sales calls that present or clarify what you are selling to your prospect. While the exact nature of your presentation will depend on your specific industry and product, the most common types of presentations are as follows:

- The written proposal
- The demonstration
- The closing interview
- The after sale follow up call

It is important to remember that, regardless of the presentation type, the prospect only needs enough information to make his buying decision. For example, most people do not need to know what grade of steel their car door is made out of before they buy it.

Many sales have been lost because the sales representative actually confused, bored, or scared the prospect by giving him too much information. You just have to answer the question, "What is in it for me?" Although the answer will be different for every prospect, if you are not able to answer this question, you need to do another fact find, not a presentation.

The Written Proposal

The written proposal is the most common of presentations in business to business sales. This is also where sales representatives make the most mistakes.

Some products are very simple or transactional in nature. Prospects for these products do not need a detailed written proposal before making their buying decision. For example, most companies do not need a quotation every time they buy paper or pens.

A common mistake here is that the sales representative will just write a price on the brochure. The problem is that this does nothing to move the sale forward, nor does it accomplish any of the objectives of a presentation discussed earlier. A more effective method would be to write the price directly on a contract or sales order. Not only does this accomplish all of the objectives, but it will save a lot of time because the sale will close much more quickly.

On the reverse, if a product is larger and more complicated, some sales representatives believe that their written proposal must be larger and more complicated as well. They believe that the higher the dollar value, the longer the quotation they need to provide. They include page after page of features and specifications, all of which is not needed for the prospect to make their buying decision. Too much information can actually slow or halt the sale, not move it forward. Most people don't need or want detailed blueprints of framing, plumbing and electrical wiring before they buy their house!

Successful sales representatives have found that templates are a huge time saver when creating proposals. All that is needed to customize the proposal for a particular prospect is to change the customer information and the financial considerations and then print! Templates also ensure that you are including all the key information necessary, but just enough of the right information so that the prospect can make a logical buying decision.

The proposal itself should be printed on your letter head. If this is not possible, ensure that your company logo and contact information such as your address, phone number and website are contained in the header and footer of each page. If time passes, and someone new in the prospect's company picks up the proposal, they should easily be able to find the information necessary to contact you.

Lastly, it has happened where prospects will rule out proposals because of spelling mistakes. They think, "If the sales representative cannot take the time to correct spelling mistakes, they probably will not take the time to service me as a customer!" Spelling and grammar do count, so take the time and use your spell checker!

The following proposal format is a template that has be used very successfully by many sales representatives. It can be used regardless of your industry or the product or service that you are selling. The main sections of the template are:

- Title Page
- Company Information
- Present Situation Assessment
- Proposed Solutions
- Financial Considerations
- Implementation Schedule & Shared Expectations
- Enclosures

The whole proposal should be no longer than 6 pages, with each section as a separate page. If possible, make it shorter by combining different sections onto the same page, but do not make it longer. Any other detailed information, if needed at all, should be included as an enclosure only, and not part of the proposal.

Title Page

The title page is the first page of the proposal. Unlike the other sections, this page of the proposal should always stand on its own, and should never be combined with other sections.

The information included on the title page should be as follows:

- The prospect's company name, using the heading "Proposal For:"
- What will be discussed in the proposal, using the heading "Subject:"
  - The subject should not be a statement like "Quotation for Widgets". It should relate directly back to your headline from your prospecting call or closing statement from your fact find interview. For example, the subject of your proposal could be "Acquiring New Customers & Increasing Revenues Through The Use Of Widgets".
- The prospect's name and title, using the heading "Prepared For:"
- Your name and title, using the heading "Presented By:"
- The date of the proposal, using the heading "Date:"

Often, the title page is your prospect's first impression of you and your company in written format. As such, it is worth the time to make it look professional.

Company Information

Prospects will only do business with companies they can trust. They need to know that you will service their needs, and that your company will be around to stand behind your products. They don't like to take risks on the unproven, and most don't like to be the first to buy a product. Before prospects can trust you, they need to know that you can do what you say you can do. Although they may not say it, your prospect is thinking, "If your company is so good, why have I not heard of you before?"

The bottom line is that everything else you say in your proposal will fall on deaf ears until you show the customer that they can trust you. In other words, before the customer will buy from you, you need to build creditability. Therefore, page two of your proposal should include information that does just that.

In this section, you should include information about your company, including what you do and who you are. It can be done in a cover letter of in bullet point format. You could include a brief company history, the number of years you have been in business, or an outline of your experience.

Another great way to build your creditability is to list some of your customers in this section of your proposal. You don't need to give complete references here, just a list of local, recognizable company names of customers who are happy to be doing business with you. You could also include some one line quotes from your satisfied customers. This list you use should be always be current and updated regularly.

This information, although just a brief one page summary in your proposal, will go a long way in building your creditability and trust in your prospect's eyes.

Present Situation Assessment

One of the biggest mistakes that a sales representative can make is that they do a great fact find, but they never refer back to what they discovered in their proposal. This means the prospect never makes the link between their problems and the sales representative's solution, and therefore they do not buy. Avoiding this is the purpose of the *Present Situation Assessment* section of the proposal.

As the name implies, here is where you discuss the prospect's current situation as discovered in the fact find. You should also assess the implications of the current situation for the customer. In other words, do not just state how things are, but also state what they mean to the customer. More specifically, the information that could be included in this section is as follows:

- List the current supplier and models of your product
- List current volumes or usage of your product
- List all current issues and problems that were discovered in the fact find
- List current financial considerations

Using the group dental plan example discussed previously, a Present Situation Assessment statement could be as follows:

- The current group dental plan is underwritten by ABC Benefit Corporation. There are approximately ten manual claims filed per month, and the average turnaround time for reimbursement 45 days. There have been complaints received from employees due to the time delay in receiving reimbursement payments once claims are filed. The result is the dental plan is not considered a valuable benefit in the employees' eyes. The total company premium for the current plan is $1000.00 per month.

As you can see, a *Present Situation Assessment* statement like the one above links the prospect's problems to the need for a solution. It is also worded so if someone is reading you proposal without ever having attended a previous fact find meeting, they should be able to understand exactly why a solution is needed and therefore why are you making your proposal in the first place.

Proposed Solution

Once you have created the need for a solution in the *Present Situation Assessment* section, then you must actually provide it in the *Proposed Solution* section.

The statements included here should be worded so they relate directly back to the problems stated previously. Every issue raised in the *Present Situation Assessment* should be addressed in the *Proposed Solution* section. Once this is complete, you can state other benefits that other customers have realized that may also be of interest to this particular prospect.

More specifically, the information that should be included in the *Proposed Solution* section is as follows:

- The product name and/or model number of the proposed solution
- The advantages of the proposed solution as they relate to the prospect's specific needs
- The advantages of the proposed solution as they relate to other challenges and problems as experienced by your other customers.

Continuing with the example from above, the proposed solution statement would read as follows:

- The proposed dental plan includes a claim card for every employee. This card is accepted by the dentist as direct payment, as opposed to the employee paying the expense up front. This completely eliminates the need to reimburse the employee. Complaints on this issue will cease, and the employees' perceived value of the dental plan will increase dramatically, providing better return on the premium dollars spent!

Please note that a *Proposed Solution* statement should not just be about a product or its feature, but should also include the prospect's benefit of that feature. Customers don't buy features, they buy the benefits they derive from those features. In this case, the claim card is the product and the direct payment to the dentist is the feature. What is of real importance to the prospect is that complaints will be eliminated, his employees will value the dental plan more, and he will get a bigger bang for his buck! In other words, he will buy from emotion but justify with the facts.

As time goes on, you will see that the same *Present Situation Assessment* and *Proposed Solution* statements can be used for different prospects, just by changing the prospect's company specifics. By doing so, you are creating your proposal template that you can use quickly and easily for all of your written proposals. You don't have to spend the time and start from scratch for each proposal. You just need to decide which points to use in which proposal based on the information discovered in your fact find.

Financial Considerations

All pricing and other investment information is contained in the Financial Considerations section of the proposal. Depending on your industry, your product, and your company's policies, this section could include some or all of the following:

- Purchase price
- Financing options and terms
- Comparison of current and proposed solution costs
- Return on Investment (ROI) analysis.
- Terms and conditions

The terms and conditions section is where you outline exactly what is included or excluded from the price. For example, you should outline whether taxes, installation and training are included or excluded in your quoted price. You should also outline how long the pricing quoted is valid. A statement such as, "Quotation is valid for 30 days. Pricing is subject to change after March 31." should be included in every proposal.

Terms and conditions are often left out of proposals by sales representatives who wrongly believe that the information is too negative to discuss with a prospect. In reality, when worded properly, the terms and conditions section can help the sales representative control the time frame and close the sale.

Many sales professionals have debated as to whether you should propose just one solution to the customer, or whether you should provide multiple options of increasing value and price. Some believe that if you have followed your sales process properly, including a thorough fact find and needs analysis, only one solution for the customer will emerge and that is all that should be proposed. Others believe that you should provide at least two options, so that the customer is choosing between option 1 and option 2, as opposed to a "yes or no" decision when you only propose one solution.

There is no right answer to this debate. Not only does this depend on your industry and your product, it also depends on your customer. Your sales manager and your colleagues can help you to decide, or you could ask your customer in the fact find if they are expecting multiple options. It is recommended however, that if you do decide that multiple options work best, you limit the number of options to three. You want to give the prospect a choice, but you don't want to give him your whole price book.

Implementation & Shared Expectations

The *Implementation & Shared Expectations* section is one of the most important sections within the proposal. Unfortunately, it is also one of the most overlooked. Not only will an *Implementation & Shared Expectations* section help to control the time of frame of the sale, more importantly, it will also help you to close the sale more quickly.

You will also have a happier customer, and it will be less stressful for you. Both you and the buyer will know exactly what needs to be done, when it needs to happen, and who is responsible for each task. Just sharing this information alone ensures a successful implementation of the proposed solution! When everything goes exactly according to plan, your customer will be very willing to provide references and referrals for you to start a new sale.

Again the information for the *Implementation & Shared Expectations* section is industry and product specific. Having said that, every proposal should include the following:

- A list of the required sales order paperwork needed to complete the sale
- Order processing time frames
- Delivery schedules and time frames
- Installation and training schedules
- Other requirements needed for implementation
- Customer responsibilities
- Date of follow up meeting after implementation

Some sales representatives believe the customer has no responsibilities in the implementation other than the signing of the paperwork. While this may be true in some industries, it is often not the case. For example, if you are selling equipment, the customer may have to have the proper electrical requirements available before installation. Or if there is operator training required, the customer has the responsibility to ensure that his staff is available on the date and time specified.

The better you think the implementation through, the smoother it will go. The smoother it will go, the better references and the more referrals you will receive when you meet the customer in the follow up meeting. Remember, as sales people, we tend to think the sale is finished when prospect signs the contract. For the customer, however, that is when he thinks the sale is just beginning.

Other Enclosures

The last section of the written proposal is the Enclosure section. Here is where you include brochures and detailed product specifications if you feel they are necessary. You will not necessarily discuss these enclosures with the customer in great detail. Instead, you will just inform him that you have included them for his reference.

Another enclosure you could include is a list of other products that your company also sells. This could instantly start a new sale!

You could also include a sheet of references listing contact information of happy customers. Many prospects won't actually end up calling them, however it builds instant creditability when you provide them unsolicited.

The Demonstration

Another type of presentation sales call is the demonstration. Depending on your industry, sometimes the customer must see, touch or try the product before purchasing. For example, most people take a car for a test drive before purchasing it, and most people do a walk through before purchasing a house.

If your product normally requires the customer to see a demonstration before purchasing, it is highly recommended that you provide a written proposal to the prospect first. Demonstrations can take a lot of planning and preparation, time of which can be better spent selling. By providing the price and terms of the sale beforehand, you may find that the demonstration is not even needed because the customer has already made their buying decision. The demonstration should just prove and confirm what you stated in your proposal, not replace the proposal itself.

A real life example of this is from a sales representative selling technical equipment. During the sales process, the customer asked the price and was told verbally "forty nine, ninety five." The prospect thought that was great, and all the arrangements were made for a demonstration before the prospect ever saw the price in writing. Support staff was even brought in from out of town for the meeting. At its conclusion, the sales representative, seeing that the customer loved the equipment, pulled out the contract and asked for the customer's signature. The sale was brought to an abrupt halt when the customer saw that "forty nine, ninety five" meant $4,995.00 to the sales representative, when she thought it only meant $49.95!

Preparation prior to the demonstration is critical. All product set up should be complete and tested long before the meeting starts. The prospect should be able to just walk in, and you should be able to start.

You also do not want any surprises during your demonstration such as new applications that require a different product set up. You must maintain control of the meeting. If something new and complicated pops up, sometimes it is best to handle it in another meeting. Besides, if you have done a proper fact find, there is no reason for any unexpected surprises.

It is also effective to show your product as close to the prospect's real situation as possible. For example, if you are selling paper folders, and your prospect only needs to fold letter sized paper, there is no need to show legal sized paper as well. Try to have a white board in the demonstration room. List the three biggest problems that your prospect is experiencing, and then demonstrate how your product solves them.

One of the biggest mistakes made by sales representatives in demonstration meetings is that they talk too much, and don't demonstrate enough. It is important to demonstrate your product working very early in the meeting as opposed to just talking about how it will work when you finally press the start button. Otherwise, you run the risk of the prospect losing interest, or even worse, giving him too much information so that he thinks your product is too complicated. People want to test drive the car, not hear all about how it was built.

You demonstration should be short and to the point. Some of the most effective demonstrations on the most complicated products could be just ten minutes long! Customer questions may take the meeting longer, but your initial showing of the product should be simple and brief to be most effective. Remember, you are demonstrating your product, not doing post sale installation training.

In some industries, it is common for prospects to ask for free, on site trials of the product for an extended period of time. Whenever possible, do not agree to these trials. Sometimes, the prospect uses these trials as a way of getting free use of a machine for an extended period of time, without ever having the intension of actually purchasing the product. Even if this is not the case, the prospect should be able to make a decision without an extended on site trial. The dealership would certainly not allow you to drive a car for a month before buying it, nor would a real estate agent allow you to live in the house before you bought it.

A better strategy for these situations is a limited time conditional order. Conditional orders are a very effective way to ensure that you are working with a serious buyer, and that the demonstration is just to confirm what has already been discussed. "Yes, Mr. Prospect, you can try this equipment before you purchase. I will post date my sales contract for one week. After that time, if the product has done what we promise it to do, we will exercise it. If not, we will just tear it up. Does that sound fair?"

If the customer says no to this, chances are he was not ready to buy at the end of the free trial demonstration anyway. However, if the sales process has been followed, including a thorough fact find with a properly fit solution, chances are that the customer will say yes. Then your trial is not merely an on-site demonstration for a prospect, it is actually operator training for a customer!

The Closing Interview

Every sale must have a closing interview before it is complete. The closing interview, however, does not have to be a separate meeting. It could also be at the end of a written proposal or demonstration meeting. Either way, every sales process should come to a logical conclusion where the prospect either accepts or rejects the proposed solution.

It has been said that closing a sale is a natural evolution to the sales process. When the sales representative follows the sales process, first with a thorough fact find and then presenting the right solution, that statement is certainly true. Even still, the sales representative must still control the closing by actually asking for the sale.

After your last sales presentation appointment, whether it is a written proposal or live demonstration, ask the following closing question: "Mr. Prospect, in your opinion, do you feel this is the right solution for your organization and that we should proceed with the order today?"

Sometimes, when the prospect does not give an immediate answer, the sales representative will start talking again. This lets the prospect off the hook because now does not have to answer the closing question. Whatever you do, make sure you have the patience to wait for the answer, no matter how long it takes. It literally might take several minutes, but the prospect might just say yes!

If the prospect says no, then it is not the right solution, and you must back up in the sales process. Seek clarification as to why the prospect feels that you do not have the right solution. You may have to resell the benefits of the solution, or you may have to rework the solution itself. Something may have been missed in the fact find, or perhaps something has changed on the prospect's side that you are unaware of. Regardless, until the prospect agrees that you have proposed the right solution, there is no point going any further

In fact, if you have followed the sales process, there is a good chance that the prospect will agree that you have proposed the right solution and will answer yes that you can proceed with the order. If you are dealing with the person with signing authority for the purchase, present the contracts for signature. "Great, Mr. Prospect. The next step is to complete the paperwork. I have the paperwork with me today for your signature."

Controlling the Time Frame of the Sale

It is common in business to business sales, especially in larger organizations, that you could be dealing with a recommender or influencer as opposed to the signer, himself. In this case, once they have agreed that you have the right solution, the next logical question becomes "Great, Mr. Prospect, what's the next step?"

Regardless of the answer, you should always respond with clarification as to the time frame of when the next step will be completed. For example, if the next step is that your contact needs to meet with someone higher in the organization, you should confirm when that meeting is going to take place, as well as what will happen after. "If you are meeting with your boss next Tuesday, I will call you Wednesday morning."

Another example is that your proposal may have to be presented to a council or board before the final decision is made. Again, the first step is to confirm that the recommender believes that you have proposed the right solution for the organization. Then you should confirm as to when the next council meeting is and that you are on the agenda. Finally, at the end of the meeting you should confirm the next step between you and your contact.

Sometimes, the customer will respond that they will call you when their internal buying process is complete and they are ready to move forward with the order. Chances are this won't happen, so you must control the time frame. You must ask, "When should I expect to hear from you?" If the prospect says, Thursday, you should confirm that if you don't hear from him by then, you will call him Friday. This way, the sale is always moving forward and more importantly, you know when.

How to Handle Objections

The answer to the closing question that sales people dread the most is the non-committal "maybe". The customer doesn't actually use the word maybe, instead they use phrases like "I want to think about it" or "I'll have a look at your quote and get back to you." The true cause of statements like these is most often not having created enough "must haves" in the fact find stage of the sales process. Having said that, sometimes things are beyond our control, and the customer really does just want to think about it.

The best way to deal with these statements is to try and find out what has been missed, and above all else, continue to control the time frame of the sale. "I can appreciate that you want to think things over, Mr. Prospect. Do you have any comments or questions, or is there anything else that I can explain to you more clearly?" Once the questions have been asked and answered, control the time frame of the sale as discussed previously by asking, "When should I expect to hear from you?"

Please note the wording as to how the prospect was asked if he had questions. If you ask your prospect, "do you understand what I have said?" it implies that it is his fault if he has questions. When you take the onus on yourself and imply that if he has questions it is because you did not explain yourself clearly, it is more likely that the prospect will actually ask the questions. He will believe that it is your fault that he did not understand, and he will be more comfortable to ask.

Other disguises for the "maybe" answer to your closing question include "I don't have the budget" or "your price is too high". Sales representatives, after taking their prospects at their word, then get frustrated when the sale still doesn't close after they offer additional price discounts.

The fact is that prospects tend to disguise their true objections as to why they won't order your product. They don't necessarily do this consciously or maliciously, sometimes prospects just don't know why they can't do business today! The sales representative cannot close the sale, not because they cannot handle the objection, but because they are handling the wrong objection.

It is the responsibility of the sales representative to help the customer buy the right solution by flushing out the true objection so that everyone can move forward. The best way to do this is to actually ignore the objection the first time the prospect says it. 'Mr. Prospect, just pretend for the moment that you did have the budget, do you believe that this is the right solution for you today?"

If the customer says no, then the budget objection was not the true objection, but just a disguise. You have to dig deeper. "Mr. Prospect, what needs to change to make this the right solution for your company?" Work with you customer to find the right solution. Remember, if the prospect does not see value in your proposal, he will not buy it, no matter what the price.

The customer could also answer your question with a response like, "Yes, it is the right solution, but I really do not have the budget!" When your customer repeats the same objection like this, then you have actually uncovered the true objection. When you have discovered the true objection, you can deal with it. For example in this case, you can work with your customer to scale back your solution to fit the budget. Bottom line is that when you deal with the true objection, you are moving the sale forward.

The "just pretend for the moment" question is a very powerful sales tool to help the customer make the right buying decision. Sometimes, you may have to ask a series of "just pretend for the moment" questions to uncover what is truly holding the prospect back. It is only when the same objection is repeated twice that you have actually discovered the true objection, and can then proceed with the sale.

Don't think of objections as obstacles. Instead, think of them as opportunities to move the sale forward.

Always Be Prepared To Make the Sale

Finally, in order to truly close the sale, you and the customer must complete your sales order paperwork. What is needed will depend on your product or service, as well as your company's order process, however below are some tips to make this go smoother for all involved:

- Whenever possible, have all the necessary paperwork filled out before you arrive at the prospect's office. This is much less stressful than having to complete the paperwork knowing that the prospect is watching you.

- Take the time and double check your paperwork beforehand. It is very embarrassing to have to go back to the customer and get things resigned because you made a mistake. If you don't have time to do it right the first time, when are you going to find time to do it right the second time?
- Always carry with you in your briefcase at least two blanks of every piece of paper a customer may ever have to sign. If you do make a mistake while in front of the customer, at least you have a backup that you can use without having to run back to your office.

The signing the sales order paperwork may be the conclusion of the sale for the sales representative, however it means that the implementation process is just beginning for the customer. Once the prospect has signed all the paperwork, you need to transition this for the customer. "Mr. Prospect, congratulations! You have made a wise business decision. It is now my responsibility to ensure that the solution is implemented as we have discussed."

The After Sale Follow-Up Call

The last type of presentation sales call actually takes place after your product or service has been delivered, and the customer is realizing the benefits of the solution. The exact timing of this interview depends on your industry, however it is recommended that you meet with the customer no more than 30 days after the implementation of the solution is complete. Any longer and the meeting will not be as productive as it should be.

The primary objective of the After Sale Follow-Up Call is to ensure that that the customer is satisfied with you and your company. Essentially, you need to confirm that the customer perceives you to have done exactly what you said you were going to do. "Mr. Customer, it has been about a month since we completed our solution. In your opinion, do you feel we accomplished what we set out to do? Are you satisfied with our product and service?"

Many sales representatives do not complete the post-sale interview at all because they fear that the customer will answer this very question negatively. If you customer is not happy, the sooner you know about it the better.

In fact, studies have shown that for every customer complaint you receive, there are probably another 29 customers that are just as unhappy, but just will not take the time to tell you. That is a lot of negative word of mouth advertising! On the reverse, it has been said that if you help an unsatisfied customer solve a problem in a timely manner, that customer will be more loyal than if the problem had never occurred in the first place. Do not leave something this important to chance. Ask you customer if he is satisfied. If he is not, fix it and do so immediately. If he is satisfied, then proceed with the call.

The next step is to ask why he is satisfied. Confirm what benefits are of most value to the customer. Also, ask the customer if you could use him as a reference for other potential customers. There will never be a better time than to ask for references than right after the customer has told you why he is so happy with you and your product.

Once the customer has confirmed that everything is running smoothly, the next objective is to ensure that the customer understands how to continue to do business with your company in the future. If applicable, any reordering procedures should be discussed, as well as service and administrative protocols. It is important that the customer knows whom to contact when, and that does not always mean that he should call you. You are the just quarterback for your company's customer service department, not the whole team.

The last, and often overlooked, objective of the After Sale Follow-Up Sales Call is to create a new sales opportunity. One way to do this is with add-on sales. "Mr. Customer, while implementing this project, I noticed that you are experiencing a service problem with your gadgets. Many of our widget customers similar to you have told us that our gadgets have eliminated that problem. I would like to investigate this further with you. Are you available next Tuesday at 10:00am, or do you prefer Wednesday at 2:00pm?"

Another way to create a new sales opportunity from a satisfied customer is to obtain referrals to completely new prospects. "Mr. Customer, as you stated, you are very happy with the benefits that you have received from our product. Are there any other companies that you know of that I should be contacting so that they can realize those same benefits? Whom should I contact? May I tell them that I was recommended by you?"

Referrals are a very powerful prospecting tool. The more that you ask for them, the more you will receive. If you think about it, whenever anyone is happy with a purchase, they love to tell their friends and associates about it. Didn't you tell someone when you bought your last car? The key to referrals is, however, that you must earn the right to ask beforehand. If you do not confirm that your client is satisfied first, you simply will not receive referrals, no matter how often you ask.

Also, it is very important that you let you customer know the result of your contact with the referral afterwards. "Mr. Customer, I just want to give you a quick phone call to thank you for your referral to Fred Smith. I contacted him today, and we will be meeting next week to discuss how I can help." Customers appreciate this type of call so much that you often will receive another referral before you hang up the phone!

A long term business relationship is much more profitable that a one shot deal. It is much easier to sell to a current customer than it is to always have to generate a new customer. By properly completing the After Sales Follow-Up Call, sales representatives will not only make their lives easier, they will also be more successful too.

Planning Your Presentation of Offers

As stated earlier, the types of presentations that you complete will depend on your specific industry, as well as the product or service that you are selling. Whether or not you need to provide written proposals or complete product demonstrations, you must prepare in advance to ensure that you are effective.

The *Presentation of Offer Planning Worksheet.xls* is shown on the next few pages. It is an Excel workbook that will help you to plan the presentation of offer sales calls required to sell your product or service.

The workbook contains the following four worksheets:

- Written Proposal Template Creation Worksheet
- Demonstration Planning Worksheet
- Closing Interview Planning Worksheet
- After Sale Follow-Up Planning Worksheet

B B SALES CONNECTIONS

Written Proposal Template Creation Worksheet

Step 1 - Title Page

Does your template title page include the following headings? Answer "Y" or "N".			Date:	
Proposal For:	Prepared For:	Presented By:	Subject:	
Subject Statement				

Step 2 - Company Information

What company information will you include in your template?	

Step 3 - Present Situation Assessment

Using the questions created on the Fact Find Creation Worksheet in Section 2, create Present Situation statements.

Statement 1	
Statement 2	
Statement 3	
Statement 4	
Statement 5	

Step 4 - Proposed Solution

Using the Presentation Situation statements created above, create Proposed Solution statements.

Statement 1	
Statement 2	
Statement 3	
Statement 4	
Statement 5	

Step 5 - Financial Considerations

Should your template include the following Financial Considerations? Answer "Y" or "N".			Purchase Price	
Financing Options	Cost Comparison	ROI Analysis	Terms & Conditions	
List of Terms & Conditions				

Step 6 - Implementation Schedule & Shared Expectations

List all of your required sales order paperwork.	
List your order processing, delivery & installation time frames and schedules.	
List your customer's responsibilites.	
List other informtion to be included.	

Step 7 - Enclosures

List enclosures to be included with your written proposal.	

B B SALES CONNECTIONS

Demonstration Planning Worksheet

Enter information in the yellow boxes to to plan for your product demonstrations.

Step 1 - Products To Be Demonstrated

List all products to be demonstrated.

Step 2 - Site Preparation

Have the products to be demonstrated been set up and tested?

Have you rehearsed the demonstration?

How long is the demonstration?

Are the supplies and materials needed for the demonstration available?

Is there a white board in the room?

Is the demonstration room neat and tidy?

Step 3 - Customer Issues

List the 3 biggest issues the customer is experiencing, and outline how they will be solved by the demonstrated products.

Problem 1

Problem 2

Problem 3

B B SALES CONNECTIONS

Closing Interview Planning Worksheet

Enter information in yellow boxes to plan your closing interview.

Step 1 - Objection Preparation

List 5 common true objections that you may receive and outline possible solutions.

Objection 1	

Objection 2	

Objection 3	

Objection 4	

Objection 5	

Step 2 - Order Processing Paperwork

List all the sales order processing paperwork required to sell your product or service in the chart below.

Form Name	Required For What Products?	Customer Signature Required or For Internal Use Only

B B SALES *CONNECTIONS*

After Sale Follow-Up Planning Worksheet

Enter information in the yellow boxes to plan your after sale follow-up call.

Step 1 - Satisfied Customer Script

Mr. Customer, it has been about | | since we |

In your opinion, do you feel we have accomplished what we set out to do?

Are you satisfied with our products and services? | | What is it that you are most satisfied with?

May I use you as a reference for other potential customers?

Would it be possible for you to put your comments into a refrence letter for me?

Step 2 - Product Reordering Procedures & Company Contacts

Mr. Customer, here is a list of other important contacts and procedures to ensue that you remain a happy customer.

Contact	Reason for Contact	Method of Contact

Step 3 - Related Products Script

Mr. Customer, while implmenting this project, I noticed that you are experiencing

Many of our customers similar to you who use | | have told us that our

has also

I would like to investigate this further with you. Are you available on | | or do you prefer

Step 4 - Referral Request Script

Mr. Customer, you have stated that you are very happy with the benefits that you have received from our

Are there any other companies that you know of that I should be contacting so that they can realize those same benefits?

Who should I contact?

May I tell tham that I was recommended by you? | | Thank you.

CONCLUSION

Closing a sale is a natural evolution to the sales process. By prospecting the right target, and completing a thorough fact find, properly presenting the right solution can only yield to the logical conclusion of closing the sale.

Although the presentation of offer stage of the sales process can include many different types of presentations, if you close one sale and then start another, you were successful. And when you have done so, you have actually helped your customer get to where he wanted to go.

One good deed leads to another.

About The Author

"Those who say it cannot be done are
usually interrupted by those already doing it."
- James Baldwin

SUSAN A. ENNS

Susan is a Managing Partner of B2B Sales Connections, having been with the firm since inception. She brings over 22 years of direct sales, management and executive level business to business experience.

Before co-founding B2B Sales Connections, Susan gained marketing, sales and general management experience in the business technology and office equipment industries. She also has experience in the group insurance industry, as well as owning and operating her own businesses. Some of her career highlights include:

- Directed two regional sales operations simultaneously to outstanding sales growth
- Increased a regional sales operation to 39% average annual sales growth over a 5 year period
- Achieved 374% of profit targets as Branch Manager
- Managed the top branch in Canada, with consistent year over year record sales results
- Operation selected as a finalist in the Better Business Bureau Torch Awards for Marketplace Ethics
- Sales Representative of the Year for two consecutive years before being promoted to sales management

Susan has received her Bachelor of Commerce (Honours) degree from the Faculty of Management at the University of Manitoba, where she was named to the Dean's Honour List in three separate years. She is also a Certified Internal ISO Auditor.

She has written the training courses for sales and sales management, created numerous automated sales tools, and as the B2B Sales Coach, she writes and edits the company's newsletters. Her work has been published in several locations numerous times and has sold on four separate continents.

For many years, Susan has volunteered on numerous executive committees of professional associations, sport leagues and clubs in which she has been a member. Participating on the Leadership Executive of the Sales Professionals of Ottawa since 2008, she has served as Marketing Lead, Vice President, and is currently the association's President. She has also been a guest lecturer at the School of Business at Algonquin College as well as a guest speaker for SPO. She is an annual participant in the Canadian Cancer Society Relay for Life, and holds multiple positions on the Volunteer Committee for the Canadian Breast Cancer Foundation CIBC Run For The Cure.

A competitive athlete from an early age, she is a Kinsmen Award Winner for Good Citizenship, Sportsmanship, and Hard Work. Now an avid golfer, she has been voted Most Sportsmanlike Player and All Star Skip in separate curling leagues.

By creating and teaching various sales training courses, coupled with the innovative creation and implementation of useful sales tools, Susan has excelled and been recognized in all areas of her personal and professional endeavors.

Other Titles from Susan A. Enns

Discover these titles from Susan A. Enns, Managing Partner of B2B Sales Connections at www.b2bsalesconnections.com

- Action Plan For Sales Success
- Action Plan For Sales Management Success
- Daily Motivational Quotes

Connect with Susan Online

Connect with Susan online at

- Website: www.b2bsalesconnections.com
- A Sales Compass: A Blog by B2B Sales Connections: http://www.b2bscblog.com
- LinkedIn: www.linkedin.com/in/SusanEnns
- Facebook: www.facebook.com/B2BSalesConnections
- Twitter: www.twitter.com/SusanEnns
- YouTube: www.youtube.com/SusanEnns
- Skype: User Name - susanenns.14

www.ingramcontent.com/pod-product-compliance
Lightning Source LLC
Chambersburg PA
CBHW051224200326
41519CB00025B/7242